"Beginning with Aristotelian v
Christian ethics, de Mingo Kar
virtues before turning to the Beatitudes. He gently moves the
reader beyond seeing the Beatitudes as corporal and spiritual
works of mercy to be performed for the sake of others. Instead he
challenges us to see the Beatitudes as pertinent virtues for the
moral life. Virtues that if cultivated help us respond to God's call
and change us over time in the image of Christ. In so doing he
connects the moral life and the life of discipleship."

— Kathryn Lilla Cox
Visiting Research Associate
University of San Diego

"The author wisely and helpfully sets the stage for his presentation
by concisely narrating the five centuries of Catholic moral theology
and its renewal in the decades around the Second Vatican Council.
In so doing, de Mingo Kaminouchi introduces readers to a wide
range of voices in Catholic moral theology, some more familiar
(Curran, Ratzinger, Fuchs, Hauerwas, Rubio, and Häring) and
others less familiar, especially voices from Spain that rarely get
a hearing among North American readers. The structure of the
book is masterful, giving teachers and students solid foundations
for an ongoing consequential discussion of Christian ethics in a
world that continues to struggle to find its own grounding for
conversations about value, character, and ethics. This introduction
is a solid grammar of Christian ethics, and it deserves to find a
home in the classrooms of North American colleges and
seminaries."

— Christopher McMahon, PhD
Professor of Theology
Saint Vincent College

"Thoroughly rooted in Scripture and history, comprehensive but
never tedious, accessible without sacrificing depth—a lucid and
engaging introduction to the beauty of the Christian story and life
lived in response to it."

— Kate Ward, PhD
Assistant Professor of Theology
Marquette University

"Athens meets Jerusalem in this splendid text that introduces students to contemporary virtue ethics. Alberto de Mingo Kaminouchi covers a great deal of ground: a survey of the history of moral theology, the Christian moral life as configuration to Christ, Aristotelian virtue ethics, and the ethics of the Beatitudes. The book is written in a lucid, engaging style that invites a response to the life of happiness it describes."

— Nickolas Becker, OSB
Assistant Professor of Theology
Saint John's School of Theology and
Seminary

"Special thanks to Liturgical Press for bringing such an eloquent translation of the signature work of Alberto de Mingo Kaminouchi into the English-speaking world. De Mingo is that rare Catholic bridge builder who spans biblical theology with theological ethics and introduces us to the grammar of virtue as we learn from revelation to be configured by Christ. Rightly he unfolds for us the beatitudes at the heart of this remarkable lesson and then concludes with an introduction to the three forms of love. I cannot recall ever such a compelling and ultimately satisfying introduction to Christian ethics. Bravo!"

— James F. Keenan, SJ
Canisius Professor
Boston College

An Introduction to Christian Ethics
A New Testament Perspective

Alberto de Mingo Kaminouchi

Translated by
Brother John of Taizé

LITURGICAL PRESS
ACADEMIC

Collegeville, Minnesota
www.litpress.org

Cover design by Monica Bokinskie. Cover photo courtesy of Getty Images.

Originally published as *Introducción a la ética cristiana*, by Alberto de Mingo Kaminouchi. © Copyright by Ediciones Sígueme S.A.U., Salamanca 2015.

Scripture text translations in this work are by the translator.

Excerpts from documents of the Second Vatican Council are from *Vatican Council II: Constitutions, Decrees, Declarations; The Basic Sixteen Documents*, edited by Austin Flannery, OP, © 1996. Used with permission of Liturgical Press, Collegeville, Minnesota.

1   2   3   4   5   6   7   8   9

Library of Congress Cataloging-in-Publication Data

Names: De Mingo Kaminouchi, Alberto, author.
Title: An introduction to Christian ethics : a New Testament perspective / Alberto de Mingo Kaminouchi ; translated by Brother John of Taizé.
Other titles: Introducción a la Ética cristiana. English
Description: Collegeville, Minnesota : Liturgical Press, 2020. | "Originally published as Introducción a la ética cristiana, by Alberto de Mingo Kaminouchi, Copyright by Ediciones Sígueme S.A.U., Salamanca 2015." | Includes bibliographical references. | Summary: "An introduction to Christian ethics which examines the New Testament through three concepts of Aristotle's ethics: happiness, virtue, and love"—Provided by publisher.
Identifiers: LCCN 2020010678 (print) | LCCN 2020010679 (ebook) | ISBN 9780814688090 (paperback) | ISBN 9780814688120 (epub) | ISBN 9780814688120 (mobi) | ISBN 9780814688120 (pdf)
Subjects: LCSH: Christian ethics. | Aristotle. | Ethics. | Bible. New Testament—Criticism, interpretation, etc.
Classification: LCC BJ1275 .D41513 2020 (print) | LCC BJ1275 (ebook) | DDC 241—dc23
LC record available at https://lccn.loc.gov/2020010678
LC ebook record available at https://lccn.loc.gov/2020010679

Contents

Introduction

From the very beginning, Christians understood that the response to the gift of faith encompasses one's entire existence. Being a Christian does not essentially mean accepting a series of ideas about God, but rather living a life transformed by the Holy Spirit in the service of the good news of God's Reign proclaimed by Jesus. "Christian ethics" is the name that we give to our reflections concerning this lived-out response to Christ.

Being a Christian is a question of practice; we learn to follow Christ by walking in his footsteps. For this reason, one of the names used by the church to refer to itself in the early days was "the Way." Christianity is not a theoretical system, but an existential response to the revelation of God in Jesus, sustained by the power of the Spirit. It is life. Theological reflection comes afterwards, trying to articulate explanatory models of what has occurred, of the way we are living and why. Moral theology is the branch of theology that is concerned with the practical dimension of faith: for this reason, "Christian ethics" and "moral theology" are synonyms.[1]

This book is an attempt to investigate the circular process established in the New Testament between faith and action, between God's revelation and the response of the believer.

---

[1] In these pages we will also use the terms "ethical" and "moral" as synonyms, following in this Marciano Vidal, *Moral de actitudes I. Moral fundamental*, Madrid 1990, 18.

Christian life can be understood as the process of transformation that welcoming the Good News of Jesus sets in motion, but this process cannot be sustained over time if there is no real change. For this reason, if believers do not collaborate by their own efforts with the action of the Holy Spirit, the force of the Gospel will ultimately be dissipated. When we do not live out what we believe, faith in the God who changes our being can end up being foreclosed.

One of the new developments that, in the past few decades, have enriched the panorama both of moral theology and of theological ethics has been the return to Aristotelian virtue-ethics, viewed as a fruitful framework to rethink morality at this time of crisis in the modern world. Such diverse men and women as the Indian economist and Nobel Prize winner Amartya Sen, the Canadian philosopher Charles Taylor and the Scottish philosopher Alasdair MacIntyre have made use in various ways of the ethical legacy of the great Greek philosopher to propose alternatives to the present situation. From differing perspectives, each of them has pointed out that the cause of the current crisis in the Western world is a cultural, economic and political system that has rejected, in the name of individual freedom, the project of a happiness shared in common with others.

Our reflection overlaps with this broad movement. From the philosophical ethics of Aristotle we will take up the key concepts of *happiness, virtue* and *love*, which are suitable to describe the dynamics of transformation proper to the Christian life. Starting with them, we will strive to sketch the profile of "faith working through love" (Gal 5:6).

The itinerary of this book is divided into two parts. The first part, made up of three chapters, sets out the theoretical framework we will use in attempting to understand Christian ethics. The first chapter offers a brief panorama of moral theology. This discipline was born as a field of studies with its own status within Catholic theology as a result of the Council of Trent (1545–1563) and underwent a radical transformation at the time of the Second Vatican Council (1962–1965). The *casuistic morality* of the period between those two councils was characterized by a focus on the law; according to this model, the task of moral theology consisted basically in applying moral norms to each concrete case. The basic problem with this way of reflecting on Christian behavior was that it produced a moral theology that, paradoxically, was not very theological. Obsessed with following the law, one could lose sight of the God who calls us to live lives of love. One of the lines of force of postconciliar theology has been to place in the foreground the relationship between God and the person and to present the Christian endeavor as a grateful response to the gift of God.

What characterizes and distinguishes Christianity from all other religious and philosophical proposals is the confession that the Son of God became flesh. Christ made our vulnerability, our flesh, a privileged locus of access to God. The cross is the supreme revelation of this disarming love. In Jesus, God comes to meet us and, without forcing us in any way, invites us to friendship with him. Accepting this call brings us into a process that will transform us into the image of Christ, towards the fullness of a new life that has already come to fulfillment in him through the resurrection. Christian ethics is the reflection on how we participate in this process through our behavior and our life. The second chapter presents this task under the title "configured by Christ."

The third chapter attempts an approximation to the three concepts of Aristotelian ethics that will serve as a guide in the second part of the book to reflect on the Christian life: *happiness*, *virtue* and *friendship*. The content that Christians give to these categories is very different from that which Aristotle assigned to them, but as a schema that articulates an understanding of human behavior, they are shown to be surprisingly useful to explain what happens to the believer who tries to respond with his or her life to the call of God.

The second half of our journey deals with the study of the Christian life using the concepts presented in the third chapter. Chapters four to six are entitled respectively "Happiness," "Virtue," and "Love." Through them we will examine the New

Testament witness of how the early Christians found happiness by taking part in the salvific plan of God that conformed them to the virtues of Christ. This faith made them part of a community in which they learned a love that excludes no one.

The chapter devoted to happiness deals with the purpose of life. The encounter with the Father, the Son and the Holy Spirit (Revelation) shows us that we are not in this world by chance. Life has a purpose: to participate in the saving plan of God. Happiness consists in beginning to experience this goal towards which we are heading and which Christ calls "the Kingdom of God."

The fifth chapter deals with the virtues. In it we explore the consequences of understanding happiness not as the possession of an external good, but as the acquisition of a form of being. For Christians, being happy does not mean enjoying possessions or pleasures but becoming like Jesus, the happy human being par excellence. For this reason, we will study in detail each one of the Beatitudes, a true compendium of the virtues of Jesus and his followers.

In the sixth chapter we will conclude by deepening our understanding of a third characteristic of Christian ethics: love. Since we are not saved all by ourselves, Jesus's project calls us to be part of a community, which is a school of loving. The New Testament shows us how the proclamation of the Kingdom is inseparable from the creation of a concrete network of brothers and sisters always open to hospitality. Being a believer means taking part in this proposal of a fraternity open to all, because no one is excluded from the love of God.

Our hope is that this journey on which we are setting out will contribute to a reflection on the beauty of the Christian life. In it, faith and works—believing and acting—are two faces of the same coin. For this reason, only by keeping them together can we do justice to what it means to respond with our entire being to God's revelation, whose Reign Jesus came to inaugurate.

PART ONE

The Theoretical Framework
of Christian Ethics

CHAPTER ONE

Broadening Ethical Reflection

From Trent to Vatican II: Casuistic Morality

Catholic moral theology as an independent discipline has a birthday: July 15, 1563. On that day, the twenty-third session of the Council of Trent was held. Canon XVIII was approved, which mandated the creation of seminaries to promote the adequate formation of candidates to the priesthood.

The principal objective of the council was to respond to the challenge of the Protestant Reformation by summoning the Catholic Church to achieve its own reform from within.

The council fathers understood that, in order to foster true renewal in the Christian people, a more and better prepared clergy was required. Until then there were no universal norms that established what types of studies aspirants to holy orders had to undertake, and many bishops ordained candidates who lacked even a minimal preparation to accomplish their ministry properly. Seminaries were designed as the key institutions to form clergy who would be better trained intellectually and more disciplined morally.

The canon of the Council of Trent set out in a concrete and precise fashion the conditions those who aspired to be seminarians had to fulfill; in addition, it expressed the lifestyle that those admitted to the seminary were required to practice and determined the characteristics of their devotional life. Finally, the canon went into the minutest details when it came to regulating their daily schedule.

Concerning the subjects to be taught in the classrooms, the canon prescribed the following:

> They shall learn grammar, singing, ecclesiastical computation, and the other liberal arts; they shall be instructed in sacred Scripture; ecclesiastical works; the homilies of the saints; the manner of administering the sacraments, especially those things which shall seem adapted to enable them to hear confessions; and the forms of the rites and ceremonies.[1]

"Moral theology" was the name given to the course that would be offered in these new centers to instruct the students in "those things which shall seem adapted to enable them to hear confessions." Thus a new theological discipline was born, incorporated into the academic curriculum for an eminently practical reason: to form the future priest to celebrate the sacrament of penance. In this respect Bernhard Häring comments:

> It is important to remind ourselves that the moral theology that most of us were taught in our seminaries twenty or thirty years ago is a rather recent product. Through fifteen centuries the Catholic Church had nothing like that. It is not "the" tradition but is one late tradition; and as we shall see, it was never unchallenged within the Roman Catholic Church. That there is nothing similar in the Orthodox or Protestant Churches is no wonder, since this type of moral theology came into being only after the great separation.[2]

Following the indications of Trent, moral theology was oriented towards finding solutions for cases of conscience in the

---

[1] Canon XVIII, in http://www.thecounciloftrent.com/ch23.htm, Decree on Reformation, ch. XI. "Ecclesiastical computation" is the science of calculating the moveable feasts of the liturgical calendar.

[2] B. Häring, *Free and Faithful in Christ: Moral Theology for Clergy and Laity*, Vol. I: General Moral Theology, New York 1978, 45.

confessional. The role of the confessor was seen as mainly that of a judge. The priest had to be prepared to discern whether the penitent had sinned and, in that case, if the fault was venial, grave or mortal. He had to determine, in addition, the number and the kind of all the mortal sins. The function of the moralist was to teach him to apply principles and norms to concrete cases in order to evaluate the sins and their gravity. For this reason, this kind of ethical reflection received the name of "casuistic morality."

Because of this, moral theology was more an examination of sin than a comprehensive study of Christian behavior, and so it left most of Christian life outside its area of interest. The works of mercy, discipleship, asceticism and mysticism continued to be part of Christian practice, but not of moral theology; at best, they were relegated to other fields of theology, when they were not simply ignored in the academic world.

A manual of Catholic morality published in 1907 in the United States describes clearly in its introduction the purpose and limits of this discipline:

> We must ask the reader to bear in mind that manuals of moral theology are technical works intended to help the confessor and the parish priest in the discharge of their duties. They are as technical as the textbooks of the lawyer and the doctor. They are not intended for edification, nor do they hold up a high ideal of Christian perfection for the imitation of the faithful. They deal with what is of obligation under pain of sin; they are books of moral pathology. They are necessary for the Catholic priest to enable him to administer the sacrament of Penance and to fulfil his other duties; they are intended to serve this purpose, and they should not be censured for not being what they were never intended to be. Ascetical and mystical literature which treats of the higher spiritual life is very abundant in the Catholic Church, and it should be consulted by those who desire to know the lofty ideals of life which the Catholic Church places before her children and encourages them to practice. Moral theology proposes to itself the humbler but still necessary task of

defining what is right and what wrong in all the practical
relations of the Christian life. This all, but more especially
priests, should know. The first step on the right road of conduct is to avoid evil; in the doing of good each will act according to his vocation and opportunities, moved and stirred
by the grace of God, who works in all as he wills.[3]

The apologetic tone of this text is obvious. In a country such
as the United States with a Protestant majority, Catholic theology
had to reply to the criticisms that Christians of the Reformation
made of Catholic morality. It is easy to read between the lines
the accusations that must have been going through the author's mind: "The 'papists' are only concerned with sin; they
are not interested in doing good. They are legalistic, obsessed
with rules." Thomas Slater replied to these objections by saying
that, in fact, moral theology does deal with sin and only with
sin, but the ethical life of Catholics goes far beyond the precepts
of moral theology: "Ascetical and mystical literature which
treats of the higher spiritual life is very abundant in the
Catholic Church," he affirms proudly.

The casuistic morality of the manuals has its usefulness, but
Christian faith would not have survived in the Catholic Church
if its moral life was limited only to what its moral theology
dealt with. Fortunately, that was not the case. The Council of
Trent also gave rise to new forms of spirituality that entailed
a renewal of Christian life. To quote Häring again:

On the one hand, a truly Catholic reform, whose most noble
representatives were, among others, St. Teresa of Avila and
St. John of the Cross, was giving the Church profound works
on a spirituality that, at least partially, continued the tradition of the great church fathers of whom we have spoken.

[3] T. B. Slater, *A Manual of Moral Theology for English-Speaking Countries*,
New York 1918, v–vi. This work was the first manual of Catholic moral
theology published in English. Normally books of this kind were written
in Latin.

On the other hand, there was developing a moral theology just for the solution of cases in the confessional. In this theology, the confessor's role was understood chiefly as a judge. Not only had he to know whether the penitent had sinned but also whether he had committed a grave sin (frequently equated with mortal sin) and to determine accurately the number and species of all these mortal sins. Such a moral theology no longer promotes the patterns of discipleship, of that righteousness that comes from God's justifying action and in loving response to his call to become ever more the image and likeness of his own mercy. All this was left out or at least left to dogmatic or spiritual theology.[4]

Too often this more elevated spirituality, which recovered aspects neglected by morality, remained restricted to small groups such as certain religious orders. The moral life of the average Christian, obliged only to keep the commandments, tended to remain cut off from the experience of a personal relationship with God, without which no Christian life can survive. Aware of this, men and women dedicated to pastoral concern for ordinary people attempted to create systems of devotional and charitable practices that gave shape to forms of popular piety able to sustain a profoundly Christian existence. Saint Alphonsus Liguori (1696–1787), considered by many the most important moralist in the period between Trent and Vatican II, devoted the best of his energies to promoting a life of prayer and Christian commitment among the most indigent populations of the South of Italy.[5]

---

[4] B. Häring, *Free and Faithful in Christ*, I, 46.

[5] Saint Alphonsus is known by theologians for his *Theologia Moralis*, arguably the most influential work of casuistic morality of all time. But he is also the author of *The Practice of the Love of Jesus Christ*, a book which shows his pastoral sensitivity. This work recommends Christian practices that go far beyond avoiding sin, the obsession of the moral theology of his day. Cf. A. Liguori, *The Practice of the Love of Jesus Christ*, Liguori MO 1999.

Despite these attempts, the true life of believers could not but feel the effects of a moral theology centered exclusively on sin. Some of its negative consequences are still alive and well today in certain forms of Catholicism:

1. *Minimalism.* An ethics centered on sin does not teach people to do good, but to avoid evil and occasions of sin. It favors a mentality that tries to do as little as possible, as long as the law is not broken, because nothing is gained by doing more than is necessary. Moreover, any unnecessary act, even if good in itself, can lead to situations of risk. When the main thing is to observe the law, moral generosity is truncated and replaced by an ethical minimalism.

2. *Legalism.* If the criterion of moral goodness lies in keeping the law, I can consider myself "good" if I do formally what is prescribed. We should not forget, however, that a merely external observance of norms can conceal a profound existential dishonesty.

3. *Atrophy of the conscience.* Like every other human capacity, moral discernment languishes if it is not exercised. Following the rules blindly creates personalities reluctant to think for themselves. When we are accustomed to seek security in the observance of the law, turning to authorities who decide for us in cases of doubt, our personal conscience remains underdeveloped and never reaches its adult stature.

4. *Guilt.* However hard we try, none of us is able to follow all the rules strictly. When this observance becomes obsessive, feelings of guilt are inevitable for having broken this or that law. In extreme cases, these feelings of guilt lead to scrupulosity, which can even go so far as to become a mental illness, a variation of the obsessive-compulsive disorder. Without going that far, some forms of living one's faith have been characterized by an unhealthy sense of guilt. Many people have reacted against this not only

by rejecting the moral law, but even by abandoning their faith.

5. *Individualism.* I have to worry first of all about saving my own soul. What others do is their problem.

6. *Idolatry of the norm.* The preconciliar treatises on moral theology hardly mentioned God at all. Certainly, they took for granted that God was the ultimate guarantee of every moral norm, but they left God out of their arguments, which went no further than the law. The result was that the moral theology of those manuals was, paradoxically, not very theological: once we have the norm to obey, God can be relegated to second place. The trees of each case of conscience kept people from seeing the forest of the person in his or her relationship to God.

It is important to point out that these negative effects are not due to the fact of employing norms or laws in moral reflection, but rather of making sin and the law the center of interest. Moral laws are very useful, especially in complex circumstances that require a concrete and urgent response; but when the law is placed at the center, Christian life loses its way, namely its orientation towards God.

The Renewal of Ethics around Vatican II

At the beginning of the twentieth century, moral theology was in urgent need of renewal to rediscover the theological lodestar it had lost. In fact, criticisms of casuistic morality were not lacking, especially in the German-speaking area. After the Second World War, such criticisms became more vocal on the part of French-speaking authors.[6]

---

[6] M. Vidal, *La Teología moral. Renovación conciliar y tareas de futuro,* in C. Floristán – J. J. Tamayo (eds.), *El Vaticano II, veinte años después,* Madrid 1985, 202.

In 1954, a book was published that gave a decisive impulse to this desire for change: *Das Gesetz Christi (The Law of Christ)*, by Bernhard Häring.[7] This was "the first complete manual of moral theology that provided an effective outlet for the 'dissatisfactions' regarding casuistic morality and the desires for renewal."[8] It became the first attempt at an "alternative manual" and a bridge that facilitated the transition from the preconciliar morality of the manuals to the renewed postconciliar morality. Its enormous success is a clear sign that it responded to an eager expectation. Even though it was a work of specialization, the first edition was sold out in a few weeks.[9] And in the following years it sold more than 200,000 copies in German and in the fourteen other languages into which it was translated.[10] It became a textbook widely used in seminaries and Catholic theological institutes in the two decades following its publication.[11]

The Law of Christ recovered the theological orientation that casuistic morality had lost. Its central idea is that Christian life is primarily the response of a believer to the call of God. God calls us in Jesus Christ, and the response to this call consists not in obedience to certain norms, but in a personal relationship that involves all the dimensions of one's life, which are put into play in concrete forms of behavior that either build us up or destroy us as persons. In this way, Häring indicated the direction in which the renewal of moral theology had to

---

[7] B. Häring, *Das Gesetz Christi: Moraltheologie dargestellt für Priester und Laien*, Freiburg 1954 (English version: *The Law of Christ: Moral Theology for Priests and Laity*, Westminster MD, 1961). Concerning Bernhard Häring, see M. Vidal, *Un renovador de la Moral católica: Bernhard Häring, C.SS.R. (1912–1998)*, Madrid 1998.

[8] M. Vidal, *Un renovador de la Moral católica*, 76.

[9] Ibid., 55. *The Law of Christ* is normally edited in three volumes, but its first edition was in a single volume, so unwieldy that it was difficult to use.

[10] V. Schnurr – M. Vidal, *Bernhard Häring y su nueva Teología Moral católica*, Madrid 1989, 24–25.

[11] M. Vidal, *Un renovador de la Moral católica*, 55.

take: a greater rootedness in the experience of an active faith, witnessed to by the New Testament.

> To keep Christian moral teaching from turning into an abstract truth, inclined to a sterile casuistry, it is necessary to root it in the very foundations of the faith. For this reason, Häring begins with the mystery of salvation, which is summed up in the central word of the Bible: *Basileia*, the Kingdom. This expresses both the "realm" as well as the "reign" of God, a realm and a power not by force, but by love. "The reign of God's love" is the most common translation by Häring. This concept and its reality—as the New Testament understands it—penetrates everything. . . . In the light of the framework "call-response," the basic realities of the Christian moral life (responsibility, conscience, sin, conversion) cover a new dimension which was lacking in casuistic morality: the dimension of Christian personalism.[12]

On January 25, 1959, Pope John XXIII surprised the world by convoking an ecumenical council, which would revolutionize the understanding that the Catholic Church had of itself and its presence in the world. Among the preparatory schemas there was one dedicated to morality, entitled *De ordine morali*,[13] conservative in outlook, which was finally discarded along with other drafts. Unlike what occurred with other topics, such as the liturgy or ecclesiology, Vatican II did not foster a specific reflection on morality; one of its main objectives, however, was precisely the renewal of the moral life of Christians. This paradox caused those analyzing the council to express different opinions. Whereas for Yves Congar, Vatican II was not a council of renewal in moral theology, since none of its documents specifically treated that topic, Bernhard Häring thought that it inaugurated a new era for morality and that each of its documents encouraged a rethinking of Catholic moral theology.

[12] Ibid., 57–58, 79.
[13] *Acta et Documenta Concilio Oecumenico Vaticano II apparando*. Series II. Praeparatoria, vol. III, Pars I, Civitate Vaticano 1969, 24–53.

Marciano Vidal, a key thinker in the conciliar renewal of moral theology in the Spanish language, considered that both were right. For him, even though one cannot speak of a council of morality, Vatican II inspired a new way of thinking about morality that favored an authentic renewal of this discipline:[14]

> The general spirit of the Council is an environment that accepts and even requires the renewal of morality. Moreover, many conciliar documents, even though they are not documents on morality as such, provide valuable contributions in this field; the importance of *Lumen gentium* for the understanding of the ecclesial dimension of morality has been recognized; the importance of *Dei Verbum* for a biblical rootedness of morality; the importance of *Sacrosanctum concilium* in relationship to the mystical and sacramental tone of all Christian activity. But where the moral dimension of the Council appears most clearly is in the pastoral constitution *Gaudium et spes*, where concrete topics are dealt with which are decisive for the life and behavior of Christians.[15]

To this general assessment of the four dogmatic constitutions—the highest-ranking documents that contained the decisions of the council—we should add that the decree on priestly formation *Optatam totius* includes a text that speaks specifically about the renewal of moral theology:

> Special care is to be taken for the improvement of moral theology. Its scientific presentation, drawing more fully on the teaching of holy scripture, should highlight the lofty vocation of the christian faithful and their obligation to bring forth fruit in charity for the life of the world. (OT 16)

As Häring himself revealed in an interview he granted at the end of his life, he was the one who composed that text at

---

[14] V. Gómez Mier, *in La refundación de la Moral católica. El cambio de matriz disciplinar después del Concilio Vaticano II*, Estella 1995, qualified this transformation as a "paradigm shift."
[15] M. Vidal, *La Teología moral*, 204–205.

the request of several bishops.[16] Since it was adopted in the final edition of the conciliar decree, it became a mandate from the highest ecclesial instance to develop our discipline in a particular direction. The moral theology of the future, therefore, has to emphasize:

- its specifically Christian character ("nourished more on the teaching of the Bible");

- its positive orientation towards fullness (it must not be limited to avoiding sin, but also "shed light on the loftiness of the calling");

- its ecclesial orientation (it must not be individualistic, but "of the faithful in Christ");

- its organic unity, centered on love and openness to the world ("bearing fruit in charity for the life of the world").

There was thus a call to go beyond casuistic morality, and the orientation that moral-theological reflection had to follow was fixed.[17] The main idea is that moral theology should not be limited to a list of sinful acts that must be avoided, but show that Christian life is a positive response of one's entire being to a call from God.

The work of Anselm Günthör, which represents one of the first manuals of moral theology published after the council, expresses this intuition in its title: *Chiamata e risposta* ("Call and Response").[18] God has taken the initiative, showing his grace through salvation history; Christians respond to this by welcoming the gift gratefully and acting responsibly in consequence. Almost all the postconciliar manuals of moral theology follow this line of thought and begin their exposition with a chapter on "biblical perspectives," in which they speak of salvation history as the context within which God's initiative in

---

[16] V. Salvoldi, *Häring: Una entrevista autobiográfica*, Madrid 1998, 119.

[17] M. Vidal, *La Teología moral*, 206.

[18] A. Günthör, *Chiamata e risposta*, Roma 1974. Cf. specially Vol. I, 117–162.

favor of human beings is revealed, and present the moral life of Christians as a response to this.[19]

In September 2008, the Pontifical Biblical Commission published *The Bible and Morality*, a document they had been working on since early 2002.[20] This text of the magisterium confirms the vision that characterized the direction followed by the moral theology of the postconciliar era: the moral activity of Christians is a response to the gift of God. God takes the initiative, offering salvation; Christians respond to this not with a merely theoretical faith, but with their entire lives.[21] The idea that the moral behavior of Christians is based on the structure "call-response" is the leitmotif of the argument of *The Bible and Morality*.[22]

Jesus said, "The Sabbath is made for man and not man for the Sabbath" (Mark 2:27). And yet, we have to recognize that, on many occasions, the church has set the law above persons. The central element of the moral renewal around the Second Vatican Council consisted in recovering the correct relationship between human beings and the Sabbath, the person and the

---

[19] For example, B. Häring, *Free and Faithful in Christ*, I, 7–27. The influential work of M. Vidal, *Moral de actitudes I. Moral fundamental*, Madrid 1990, does not begin with a chapter on Bible and morality, but deals with the biblical basis of every topic mentioned.

[20] Pontifical Biblical Commission, *The Bible and Morality: Biblical Roots of Christian Conduct*, Vatican City 2008, http://www.vatican.va/roman_curia/congregations/cfaith/pcb_documents/rc_con_cfaith_doc_2008 0511_bibbia-e-morale_en.html.

[21] K. Stock, "Bibbia e morale: Il recente documento della Pontificia Commissione Biblica," in *Parola di Dio e morale. Atti della giornata di Studio Accademia Alfonsiana, Roma, 20 novembre 2008*, Roma 2008, 61–63. This is a lecture by Klemens Stock, the secretary of the Pontifical Bible Commission, during the presentation of the document *The Bible and Morality* in the Alphonsian Academy.

[22] It is divided into two sections. The first retraces the principal phases of the history of salvation in the Old and New Testaments, showing how in each of them the structure *call-response* is realized. The second presents some criteria, found in the Bible, that can guide moral reflection and help to find solutions to current problems.

law. The moral life cannot consist simply in keeping the law, but rather in responding to God's call. Rules have their function, of course, but they must always be subordinated to the fundamental relationship between the believer and his or her Lord. The council urged Catholic morality to show, as its primary task, that the Christian life is a response to God's gift. The objective it assigned was to recover the theological context of morality, the vertical dimension that connects Christian activity with its source in God.

Going Deeper Leads to Broadening

The proposal of the proponents of renewal to go beyond casuistic morality by recovering the theological character of moral reflection quickly encountered critical voices, and ones that did not necessarily come from the most conservative sector. In fact, some theologians committed to the renewal of Catholic ethics exposed the problematic aspects of a moral theology that claimed to be based to such an extent on revelation.

Josef Fuchs, professor of moral theology at the Gregorian University, in an article published in 1970, questioned the idea that Christian morality has a specific content and affirmed that its content was "simply human," distinguished as Christian only by its intentionality.[23] Fuchs and other theologians, who came to be known as the "autonomy school," argued that Christian revelation did not provide new norms for ethics. Christians were therefore not morally obliged to do different things from what other human beings do; the content of ethics

---

[23] J. Fuchs, *Gibt es eine spezifisch christliche Moral?* Stimmen der Zeit 185 (1970). Cf. A. Auer, *Autonome Moral und christlicher Glaube*, Düsseldorf 1984. A good selection of documents on both sides of the debate is found in C. E. Curran – R. A. McCormick (eds.), *Readings in Moral Theology. No. 2: The Distinctiveness of Christian Ethics*, New York 1980. The article by Fuchs came from a lecture given by the author in Zurich in 1968.

was the same for all and the knowledge of what we are required to do was accessible to any rational being. These theologians were men involved in ethical dialogue with non-believers, especially with secular humanism. How could the validity of Christian moral norms be shown in debate in the public forum, if they were based on a revelation unacceptable for conversational partners who did not share the Christian faith?

Controversy was the order of the day. On the one hand there was the "autonomy school," already mentioned, that defended the absence of any specific content in Christian morality. On the other, there was a group that became known as the *Glaubensethik*, "the ethics of faith," which maintained that "apostolic moral exhortation is not a moralizing appendage the contents of which could be changed, but is the concrete designation of what faith is and is therefore linked indissolubly with its central point."[24] Faith is the core that gives form to Christian life and it has to be expressed in behavior; it is not a motivation that simply decorates a life that is, in other respects, indistinguishable from that lived by non-believers.

The debate led to a division in the theological community. Häring, who shared a sensibility and common tasks with Fuchs,[25] expressed from the outset his astonishment at the

---

[24] J. Ratzinger, *Magisterium of the Church, Faith, Morality*, in C. E. Curran – McCormick, *Readings in Moral Theology. No. 2*, 183. I have changed the words "apostolic preaching" in this English translation with my words "apostolic moral exhortation," which I think better render in English the German expression *"apostolische Paraklese"* in the original text. J. Ratzinger, *Kirchliches Lehramt – Glaube – Moral*, in J. Ratzinger, *Prinzipien Christlicher Moral, unter Mitarbeit von Heinz Schürmann und Hans Urs von Balthasar*, Einsiedeln 1975, 59. *"Paraklese"* is the German transliteration of the Greek New Testament word *"paraklēsis,"* which means "moral exhortation."

[25] Both, for instance, were part of the Pontifical Commission for the Study of Population, the Family and Birth (1963–1966), and both helped to draft the final report defending the licitness of so-called artificial methods of contraception, which was rejected by Paul VI.

claims of the "autonomy school." He considered "unacceptable the idea that the moral teaching of the New Testament did not contribute any new content to mere natural reason except for a new motivation."[26] From his point of view, the authors of the autonomy school did not understand the profound change of direction that he proposed towards a morality of true Christian freedom; they were still following the old paradigm of a morality built around moral norms with the intention of controlling consciences by means of the law.[27]

The discussion degenerated into a fierce battle. Amidst the heat of the debate, serious misunderstandings arose due to the ambiguity in the use of key terms such as "content" and "intentionality," and exaggerated and unfair judgments were exchanged.[28]

In reality, beneath the label of *Glaubensethik* were grouped theologians with different outlooks. The most radical, such as Heinz Schürmann, affirmed the existence of specifically Christian moral norms that were directly revealed by God.[29] The position of Joseph Ratzinger also fell within the *Glaubensethik*, although it was much more nuanced. Ratzinger admitted that the elements of Christian morality could proceed, even entirely, from other traditions. This meant that the newness of Christianity did not consist in producing new moral norms unknown

[26] B. Häring, *Moralverkündigung nach dem Konzil*, Bergen-Enkheim 1966, 72.

[27] Id., *Free and Faithful in Christ*, I, 23–25.

[28] V. MacNamara, *Faith and Ethics*, Washington DC 1985, 57.

[29] H. Schürmann, *Die Frage nach der Verbindlichkeit der neutesstamentlichen Wertungen und Weisungen*, in Ratzinger, *Prinzipien Christlicher Moral*, 9–39. Schürmann was conscious that not everything that appears in Sacred Scripture as a commandment can be applied today as a moral norm. He stated that it was the role of the church to examine the revealed texts in order to discern which of the norms possessed permanent value and which ones had to be seen as the result of a specific historical situation. As a "simple exegete," however, he considered himself incompetent to list those norms valid for all time.

in other cultures and religions, but "in the new overall conception (*Gesamtgestalt*) into which man's quest and aspiration was directed by faith in the God of Abraham, in the God of Jesus Christ."[30] Rather than in a norm taken by itself, what is specific to Christianity is the figure (*Gestalt*) that describes the whole of the moral life. Dietrich Bonhoeffer expressed a similar idea, decades earlier in his *Ethics*, a book left unfinished by his violent death:

> Ethics as formation (*Gestaltung*) is possible only on the basis of the form of Jesus Christ present in Christ's church. *The church is the place where Jesus Christ's taking form (gestaltwerden) is proclaimed and where it happens.* The Christian ethic stands in the service of this proclamation and this event.[31]

Here we have a definition of theological ethics that looks beyond the individual and thus acts towards the life of the ecclesial community, created to express the presence of Christ in human history through the sum total of what she is and does. This is what is specific to Christianity, and what cannot be perceived adequately in a morality that applies only to rules and to individual acts.

In reading the New Testament, we see that Jesus allots his followers a series of tasks. After Easter, the disciples of Jesus, animated by the Holy Spirit, would undertake specific prac-

[30] J. Ratzinger, *Magisterium of the Church, Faith, Morality*, 177. In the original German text: "Die christliche Originalität besteht vielmehr in der neuen Gesamtgestalt, in die das menschliche Suchen und Ringen von der orientierenden Mitte des Glaubens an den Gott Abrahams, an den Gott Jesu Christi." J. Ratzinger, *Kirchliches Lehramt – Glaube – Moral*, 48–49.

[31] D. Bonhoeffer, *Ethics*, Works, Vol. 6, Minneapolis 2009, 102. Original text: "Ethik als Gestaltung ist nur möglich aufgrund der gegenwärtigen Gestalt Jesu Christi in seiner Kirche. *Die Kirche ist der Ort, an dem das gestaltwerden Jesu Christi verkündigt wird und geschieht.* Im Dienst dieser Verkündigung und dieses Geschehens steht die christliche Ethik" (*Ethik*, München 1998, 90; italics in original). Note the importance of the term "*Gestalt*" (configuration) in both Bonhoeffer's and Ratzinger's visions of Christian ethics.

tices destined to make the Risen Christ present in the world: announcing conversion, forming communities, celebrating the Eucharist, assisting the needy, confronting the violence around them with non-violence, etc.

Christian revelation does not discover moral laws that non-believers cannot follow. In this respect the "autonomy school" was correct. One cannot say, however, that it proposes a moral life materially indistinguishable from that of other human beings, distinct only by its inner motivation. The debate about the specificity of Christian ethics teaches us that the movement of deepening that was asked of moral theology—presenting Christian activity as a response to God's call—was only possible if there was simultaneously a widening of the field of vision. If morality was meant to "show the greatness of the vocation of the faithful in Christ," as the council asked, it could not continue to be just a science of acts. In this respect Norbert Rigali writes:

> Since the *humanum* or *morale* is primarily the *vita humana*, not the *actus humanus*, contemporary ethics must understand itself much more than did traditional moral theology, as a science directly concerned with *vita humana*, which can speak legitimately about the *actus humanus* only in this explicit context. . . . Moral theology must redefine itself today as a science of the Christian life and must transform itself into a new kind of science.[32]

Christian Ethics as Grammar

The theologians of the autonomy school were motivated by the necessary and the noble concern to establish a dialogue with non-believers in moral matters. Seeking a convergence in ethical questions, they accepted the establishment of a dichotomy between content and intention. But this way of describing

---

[32] N. J. Rigali, *The Uniqueness and the Distinctiveness of Christian Morality and Ethics*, in *Moral Theology: Challenges for the Future. Essays in Honor of Richard A. McCormick*, New York 1990, 116–117.

a moral act prevents us from perceiving the internal logic of Christian activity. The task that we are undertaking here is different: we want to try to understand Christian life from within the dynamisms that animate it. We want to describe, however tentatively, the grammar of Christian ethics through a study of the primordial texts of this tradition, those collected in the New Testament.

Christianity is not a theory that we first have to understand and from which only then, in a second moment, we can deduce practical consequences. It is true that understanding something better favors a more perfect way of acting, but it is not less certain that, in order to understand certain truths of the faith, we first have to live in a certain way.

Convictions and practices exist in a circular relationship: each one emerges from the other and neither of the two can be considered as absolutely prior. We learn to be Christians not only, or mainly, by acquiring certain ideas, but by living what we believe and believing in what we live. Stanley Hauerwas has compared the process of becoming a Christian to learning a language. It takes a lot of time and practice to master a language. It is not enough to study the grammar and memorize vocabulary; you have to practice speaking it and listening to it, reading and writing. In the same way, to become a Christian it is not enough to have clear ideas; it is not a matter only of acquiring certain concepts, but of molding one's entire being for a new way of life: "To speak well, to talk right, requires that our bodies be habituated by the language of the faith."[33]

We can understand Christian ethics as the study of the grammar of this language. There are speakers who are unable to formulate the grammatical rules that regulate the language with which they communicate, since knowing these norms explicitly is not required to speak a language, but studying the grammar does help us to master it better. In the same way, it

---

[33] S. Hauerwas, *Learning to Speak Christian*, London 2011, 87.

is not necessary to know Christian ethics to act in a Christian manner, but to learn ways of formulating how Christian convictions are expressed by means of behavior accords us intellectual satisfaction and helps us to "speak the Christian language better." We must not fool ourselves for all that: the role of moral theology will always be secondary, since being a Christian is a matter of practice. We become Christians when we acquire, by a series of practices, the form of being proper to disciples of Christ.

The purpose of this book is to understand better how Christian activity is related to the revelation that we have received by faith. This way of approaching Christian ethics, which gives priority to "faith seeking understanding," does not exclude dialogue with those who profess other religions or do not practice any. On the contrary: we think that the time has come when interreligious dialogue must go beyond a coexistence based on the acceptance of the common norms of a civil ethics; we have to take steps towards a deeper understanding of the inner articulation of every religious or humanistic tradition. Even if what we are writing here is meant above all to help believers to understand themselves better, we cherish the hope that it can also serve as an invitation to non-Christians to get to know us better.

In the following pages we will attempt to outline the *moral grammar* of Christian life starting from the texts of the New Testament. The conceptual scheme that will help us to interpret them is the ethics of Aristotle, the basic elements of which we will expose in the third chapter. Beforehand, however, we will try to understand more deeply what it means, in Bonhoeffer's words, to be configured by Jesus Christ.

CHAPTER TWO

Configured by Christ

A New Model of Revelation

The basic intuition that caused postconciliar morality to go beyond the casuistic paradigm in vigor until then was the understanding of the Christian life as a response to God's call. The task of moral theology could not continue to be merely the study of the application of norms to the concrete circumstances of each case. The renewal set into motion by the council undertook the program of fostering a moral theology "nourished more on the teaching of the Bible," which would emphasize more strongly how the life of believers, in all its breadth and depth, is configured as a response to the gift of revelation.

Another of the great changes made possible by the Second Vatican Council was the way revelation was understood. The question that most interested the Roman theologians charged with drafting the preparatory schema for the conciliar document on revelation was the old debate between Catholics and Protestants about the "material completeness of Scripture." One of the maxims of the Protestant Reformation is *sola Scriptura*: everything necessary for salvation is found in the Bible. The Catholic Church, on the other hand, has always affirmed that revelation is not only communicated through Scripture, but also through Tradition. The theologians who prepared this theme for the conciliar debate wanted the "material incompleteness of Scripture" to be defined once and for all, in other words, that there are truths of revelation that are found not in the Bible, but in Tradition.

They called their document *De fontibus revelationis*, "On the sources of revelation." The proposal encountered the resistance of one of the most important currents of renewal that had converged at the council: the ecumenical movement. Defining the incompleteness of Scripture would have made reconciliation with Lutherans and other Protestant denominations impossible. The resistance was successful and the preparatory schema was rejected.[1] This unleashed a great crisis, since nobody knew what to replace it with or how far to go. The council even contemplated eliminating the theme of revelation from its debates. Finally it was determined that the absence of a document on this fundamental topic was unacceptable. After a long process of elaboration, the "longest and most laborious of all the conciliar texts produced by Vatican II," the dogmatic constitution *Dei Verbum* was promulgated by Paul VI on November 18, 1965.[2]

The need to go beyond the dilemma stirred up by the preparatory schema *De fontibus revelationis* brought the council to

---

[1] On November 20, 1962, the question was voted on as to whether *De fontibus revelationis* would be used as a text for the conciliar debates. The result of the vote was 1368 votes in favor of abandoning the text completely against 822 defenders of continuing the debate. According to the rules, 105 votes were still lacking to reach the two-thirds necessary to reject the schema. John XXIII, with great common sense and after having spent the entire night in prayer—according to the confidence of his Secretary of State—communicated his decision the next day: the text should be completely reworked by a mixed commission including members of the Theological Commission and of the Secretariat for Unity, before returning it to the council floor. Cf. J. W. O'Malley, *What Happened at Vatican II*, Cambridge MA 2008, 127–159.

[2] Cf. S. Pié i Ninot, *Tratado de Teología fundamental*, Salamanca 2006, 663; cf. J. Ratzinger, "Dogmatic Constitution on Divine Revelation: Origin and Background," in *Commentary on the Documents of Vatican II*, New York 1967, 155–166.

a fundamental reconsideration of the nature of revelation. In this process, the propositional model of revelation that had prevailed since the Council of Trent was felt to be inadequate.[3] The councils of Trent and Vatican I understood revelation, above all, as God's handing over to the church a deposit of dogmatic and moral truths; the magisterium, as the guardian of these propositions and norms, had to ensure their preservation against the errors of each age and administrate an understanding of them to the faithful through catechisms and other means of instruction. In this model of revelation understood as doctrine, faith consisted above all in an acceptance of certain truths that had to be believed.

Dei Verbum represented a revolution in this way of understanding revelation. The propositional model that had prevailed until then gave way to another model, a personalist one.[4] In its first chapter, dedicated to considering what revelation is, *Dei Verbum* affirms: "It pleased God, in his goodness and wisdom, to reveal himself and to make known the mystery of his will (see Eph 1:9), which was that people can draw near to the Father, through Christ, the Word made flesh, in the holy Spirit, and thus become sharers in the divine nature" (DV 2).

The key word here is *seipsum*, "himself." The content of revelation is God himself. God reveals "himself" and invites us into a personal relationship; he does not merely reveal contents of information, but enters into a personal relationship with the believer. To confirm this meaning of revelation as an encounter between persons, the same paragraph of the dogmatic constitution affirms: "By this revelation, then, the invisible God (see Col 1:15; 1 Tim 1:17), from the fullness of his love, addresses men and women as his friends (see Ex 33:11; Jn 15; 14-15), and lives among them (see Bar 3:38), in order to invite

---

[3] Cf. S. Pié i Ninot, *Tratado de Teología fundamental*, 245–251.

[4] The American theologian Avery Dulles coined the phrase "models of revelation" in a book of that title (Maryknoll 1992). The critical evaluation of the model of "revelation as doctrine" can be found on pp. 36–52.

and receive them into his own company" (DV 2). In the council's way of thinking, welcoming revelation does not consist above all in assenting to propositions or in complying with certain norms, but in entering into a personal relationship with a God who is seeking our friendship. This is not to deny, of course, that this relationship entails a series of beliefs and truths, but these remain secondary with respect to the mysterious but real encounter between the persons of the Trinity and every human being.

Like all the great intuitions of Vatican II, the personalist model of revelation was not an innovation, but a "return to the sources." The reader of the Bible can appreciate that this is not a book of doctrinal propositions; the Old Testament tells the story of a living relationship between God and his people Israel, and in the gospels we contemplate the encounter of the disciples and others with Jesus Christ. In the New Testament letters and in the Acts of the Apostles, we see how the presence of the Holy Spirit activates a community of believers that has placed its trust in the Risen Christ. This biblical narrative and personalist attitude prevails as well in the church fathers and in the theology of the first millennium. Even when the doctrinal aspect of the faith is emphasized—with the apparition of the scholastics in the West at the beginning of the second millennium—we encounter beautiful phrases like this one from Thomas Aquinas: "The act of believing does not terminate in the proposition but in the reality of God himself."[5]

One of the practical consequences of the promulgation of *Dei Verbum* was the entrance of the Bible into the daily life of Catholics. As a reaction to the Protestant Reformation, the post-Tridentine Catholic Church had restricted the access of Sacred Scripture to the faithful. Vatican II transformed this situation, encouraging all to read the sacred texts and ordering Catholic institutions to work for its diffusion. Over the last

---

[5] *"Actus credentis non terminatur ad enuntiabile, sed ad rem,"* Summa theologiae, II–II, q. 1.

decades, the Bible has become a book so present in Catholic parishes and families that it is hard for the younger generations to believe that before the 1960s, it was a book almost unknown to Catholics.[6] What is less known, however, is that Vatican II invited Catholics to read and interpret the Bible starting from a specific understanding of revelation. In this vision, the Gospel is not only seen as "the source of every salvific truth and every moral rule" as Trent affirmed, but especially as that place in which it is possible to have a living encounter with the God of Jesus Christ. The Bible is not understood primarily as a deposit of information about God, but as the privileged witness to the long history of God with his people and as an instrument that makes possible a present and living encounter with the mystery of the Father, Son and Holy Spirit.

Christology and Morals

In the Christian outlook, the Bible has an important place in revelation, but it is not the center; this is occupied by Jesus Christ, the Word made flesh. When God wanted to communicate with humanity, the "word" he spoke was not a text but a person, Jesus, a human being.

We read in the Letter to the Hebrews: "God spoke in many and varied ways in the past to our ancestors through the prophets, but in these final days he spoke to us through his Son, whom he made heir to all things and through whom he also created the universe" (Heb 1:1-2).

Commenting upon these verses, Saint John of the Cross wrote, "That which God formerly spoke to our fathers through

---

[6] In spite of the exaggerations that pervade its pages, George Barrow, *The Bible in Spain: Journeys, Adventures, and Imprisonments of an Englishman, in an Attempt to Circulate the Scriptures in the Peninsula*, London 1843, is a testimony to how much the Catholic clergy resisted the diffusion of the Bible in that country. The book tells of the adventures and misadventures of its author, an English Bible salesman, during his journeys in Spain between the years 1835 and 1840. It was translated into Spanish by Manuel Azaña, President of the Second Spanish Republic.

the prophets in many ways and manners, now, finally, in these days He has spoken to us all at once in His Son. The Apostle indicates that God was as it were mute, with no more to say, because what He spoke before to the prophets in parts, He has now spoken all at once by giving us the All Who is His Son."[7]

In fact, what God had to communicate to us is his Son. Christ is the definitive Word of God. Precisely here is rooted the basic difference between the way in which Christians understand revelation and Islam. For Muslims, the center of revelation is occupied by a text; the God of Islam is absolutely transcendent and it is unthinkable that God would lower himself by coming to earth and becoming incarnate. When Allah, the Merciful One, wished to communicate with human beings, he did so by means of a text, the Quran, dictated in Arabic. Muhammad occupies an essential place in this process, but one always subordinate to the text, the authentic Word of God. In Christianity, the roles are reversed: Christ is found at the center of revelation. He is the Word. The Bible has a special place alongside him, but always secondary and as a witness.

The new perspective on revelation promoted by Vatican II likewise determines another way of understanding morality. If being a believer means complying with the truths revealed by God and guarded by the Church, then a casuistic morality, concerned to apply to each concrete situation the moral norms that can be deduced from this truth, is relevant; but if the object of revelation is a God who reveals "himself" in the figure of Christ and who wants to establish a personal relationship with every human being, then the focus of attention of moral theology has to be centered on the person who responds to this revelation with his or her entire life.

The surpassing of casuistic morality is nourished by the teaching of Holy Scripture on this deep level and responds to

---

[7] John of the Cross, *Ascent to Mount Carmel* II, 22, 4. English trans. Kieran Kavanaugh, O.C.D., and Otilio Rodriguez, O.C.D., Washington DC 1979.

the call to place the person at the center of its reflection. It contemplates moral life in the context of a revelation that is now understood as a dialogue between God and humanity. Human acts continue to be important, of course, but always with reference to a human being who is on pilgrimage, seeking God through his or her existence. The essential question of moral theology will not be *"What* must I do?" but *"Who* must I be, what does the Lord want me to be?"[8]

Norbert Rigali has written that "moral theology should be a science that seeks to relate Christology to the moral lives of Christians."[9] Christians experience a dynamic transformation undertaken by the Holy Spirit; to be Christian is to be configured by the definitive revelation of God that took place in Jesus Christ—in his teachings, his life and his being. It is precisely here that Jesus presents himself as a question.

But What Jesus?[10]

William Spohn, one of the theologians who has contributed most to establishing connections between New Testament studies and Catholic moral theology, tells that when he told a professor of New Testament that he was writing a book about Jesus and ethics, the professor replied, half-jokingly and half-seriously, "But what Jesus?"[11]

---

[8] B. Häring, *Free and Faithful in Christ: Moral Theology for Clergy and Laity*, Vol. I: General Moral Theology, New York 1978, 85.

[9] N. J. Rigali, "Christ and Morality," in C. E. Curran – R. A. McCormick (eds.), *Readings in Moral Theology. No. 2: The Distinctiveness of Christian Ethics*, New York 1980, 113.

[10] This section is taken from my presentation "Los rostros de Jesús: Evangelio, historia y dogma," presented at the III International Biblical Congress of the Spanish Bible Association (Seville, September 3–5, 2012) and published in C. Bernabé (ed.), *Los rostros de Dios. Imágenes y experiencias de lo divino en la Biblia*, Estella 2013, 223–233.

[11] W. C. Spohn, *Go and Do Likewise: Jesus and Ethics*, New York 1999, 9. Spohn is also the author of the very useful book *What Are They Saying about Scripture and Ethics?* New York 1995.

The last decades have seen a real avalanche of studies about the historical figure of Jesus, which have proposed an enormous amount of different images. Some of them can be seen as complementary, offering different perspectives on a rich and complex personality. Others, however, are incompatible with one another. The proliferation of different opinions concerning who Jesus was may not be a problem for those who remain on the level of pure historical speculation, but if, as Christians, we want Christ to give shape to our lives, we need to know at least the main lines of who Christ was and how to understand his life.[12]

It is obvious that there is only one Jesus, who was born of Mary, grew up in Nazareth, preached in the villages of Galilee and was crucified in Jerusalem. Christians affirm that this man, this Jew of the first century, rose from the dead and we confess him to be the Son of God. But how can we get to know him? Untangling the complex mess of the various figures of Jesus produced by historical investigation in the last two centuries is not an easy task.[13] In order not to get lost on the road of our investigation, we must evaluate the place occupied in our faith by the witness of the gospels, but without losing sight, on the

[12] It is helpful to remember here that this was the serious problem that led Pope Benedict XVI to write his book *Jesus of Nazareth*. Faced with the perplexity of believers confronted with so many contradictory visions of Christ, he commented, "All these attempts have produced a common result: the impression that we have very little knowledge of Jesus and that only at a later stage did faith in his divinity shape the image we have of him. This impression has by now penetrated deeply into the minds of the Christian people at large. This is a dramatic situation for faith, because its point of reference is being placed in doubt: intimate friendship with Jesus, on which everything depends, is in danger of clutching at thin air." J. Ratzinger, *Jesus of Nazareth: From the Baptism in the Jordan to the Transfiguration*, London 2007, xii.

[13] Cardinal Gianfranco Ravasi, President of the Pontifical Council for Culture, even went to the point of stating that "the best way of guiding the non-technical reader in the midst of this forest [of interpretations of Jesus] seems to me to be narrative." Two good examples of this pedagogical technique are A. Puig i Tàrrech, *Jesús: una biografia*, Barcelona 2005, and J. A. Pagola, *Jesús: aproximación histórica*, Madrid 2007.

one hand, of the dogmatic statements of the church about him and, on the other, the acquisitions of modern historical investigation. Only in this way will we be able to avoid the danger of both a fundamentalist reading of the bible texts and a skepticism that leads believers to "clutch at thin air."[14]

The "Historical Jesus"

The story of the modern investigation concerning the historical Jesus[15] began in 1778 with the publication of an essay entitled *"Von dem Zwecke Jesu und seiner Jünger"* ("The Aims of Jesus and His Disciples") by Hermann Reimarus (1694–1768). For the first time a scholar defied the common belief that the image of Jesus transmitted by the four gospels corresponded to reality. Reimarus affirmed that the disciples of Christ had aims radically different from those of Jesus, and added that, for this reason, the gospels had to be read critically in order to salvage the true image of Christ buried beneath a text that did not reflect the original intention of its protagonist. Reimarus believed that he had discovered in Jesus not the Son of God proclaimed by the New Testament, but an obscure Jewish prophet who announced the definitive inbreaking of the Kingdom of God and ended up being crucified by the Romans. According to Reimarus, the disciples transformed this failure into a victory, inventing the resurrection and propagating the myth of a divine being who had returned from the dead.

Reimarus's work, edited posthumously by the philosopher Gotthold E. Lessing—the author did not dare to publish it during his lifetime—found an echo in the intellectual climate of the time. The idea that one could recover scientifically the figure of Jesus held captive for centuries by the churches at-

---

[14] Ibid.

[15] For a more complete overview, cf. R. Aguirre, "Estado actual de los estudios sobre el Jesús histórico después de Bultmann," *Estudios Bíblicos* 54 (1996); M. J. Borg, *Jesus in Contemporary Scholarship*, Valley Forge PA 1994.

tracted the attention of the German thinkers involved in the Enlightenment.

The result is what came to be called the *First Quest* of the historical Jesus. In the "lives of Jesus" published during the nineteenth century, Jesus was presented as a kind-hearted moralist who tried to communicate to his followers universal ethical values such as love, integrity, respect and tolerance. The Kingdom of God that he preached was only a metaphor, a framework to support all these values, and the miracles mentioned in the gospels were interpreted as false perceptions of natural phenomena or pure inventions of Christ's disciples. The result was a watered-down image of Jesus that was acceptable to the rationalism extolled by the nineteenth-century bourgeoisie, at a time when any political content that would call into question the projects of social and colonial domination that the elites of the Western powers were undertaking was absent.

With the publication of his *Geschichte der Leben-Jesu-Forschung* ("History of Life-of-Jesus Research") in 1906,[16] Albert Schweitzer brought an end to this first stage of the investigation. In this work, the German exegete studied the "lives of Jesus" that the liberal investigation of the nineteenth century had produced and concluded that those works, despite their claims to be scientific, did not offer an objective portrait of the historical figure of Jesus of Nazareth, but were rather a mere reflection of the spirit of the times. The publication of this study coincided with the beginning of a new intellectual climate different from that predominant in the Belle Époque. The new period was characterized by a crisis of confidence in human progress and the powers of reason, ideas that were reinforced by the catastrophe that the First World War represented for humanity. In this sense, the influence of Schweitzer's book during the first half of the twentieth century was such that many faculties

---

[16] A. Schweitzer, *The Quest of the Historical Jesus*, Minneapolis 2001. Originally published in German, in 1906.

of Protestant theology almost entirely abandoned any investigation of the historical Jesus, which had previously been so thriving.[17]

Scholars of the history of this investigation have qualified this period as a kind of *neo-conservative moratorium* on studies of the historical Jesus. In the exegesis of the New Testament, the great figure of the moment was Rudolf Bultmann, who defended not only the limited knowability of the historical Jesus, but also its total irrelevancy for faith: the important thing was to believe in Christ, the Son of God. Giving new life to the Lutheran maxim *sola fides*, Bultmann advocated an attachment to the "Christ of faith" that excluded any dependence on the "Jesus of history."

This moratorium was interrupted by the *New Quest*, launched by some of the best disciples of Bultmann who rebelled against their teacher in the 1950s and 1960s.[18] The authors of this second wave of studies on Jesus reclaimed for Christian theology the inseparability between the Jesus of history and the Christ of faith. They affirmed, *contra* Bultmann, that without a basis in the Jesus of history, Christianity remains suspended in a void and is exposed to all sorts of manipulations. They were not speaking of a mere possibility, since Protestant churches and theologians grouped under the banner "*Deutsche Christen*" spoke of the anti-Jewish Jesus extolled by the Nazis. The attainments of this second stage of the investigation in the field of history were not, however, particularly relevant.[19]

---

[17] Catholic theology in the nineteenth century did not integrate the scientific methods of Bible study that had developed during that century in the Protestant world. The few exegetes who dared to enter into dialogue with these currents of thought around the year 1900 were accused of modernism and reduced to silence.

[18] The beginning of this new investigation is usually dated from a lecture given by Ernst Käsemann in 1953 entitled "The Problem of the Historical Jesus." Cf. E. Käsemann, *Essays on New Testament Themes*, London 1964, 15–47.

[19] G. Bornkamm, *Jesus of Nazareth*, Minneapolis 1995.

In the 1980s, the work of North American scholars inaugurated the "Third Quest." During the last two decades of the twentieth century, many studies were published both for scholars and for the general public on the image of the man Jesus that could be discovered through science and history.

The Third Quest was characterized by its great optimism concerning the possibility of attaining a broad and sure knowledge of the historical Jesus, something unheard of since the nineteenth century. In addition, many of the authors of this tendency affirm that they surpass previous investigators in three basic points: first, the knowledge of *new texts* discovered in the mid-twentieth century, especially the Dead Sea manuscripts and the Gnostic codices of Nag Hammadi;[20] second, the *archeological excavations in the Holy Land* which, combined with sociological models, allow a better reconstruction of the social world at the time of Christ; third, a greater objectivity, due to the fact that the investigators of this third wave worked mainly in universities in the United States and the United Kingdom who, unlike their colleagues in German theological centers, are free from the doctrinal control of denominational schools of theology. This third point is debatable, since a lack of objectivity is not a monopoly of believers of a particular denomination; in fact, the greater freedom of investigation that these scholars enjoy in principle does not make them immune to ideological positions.

Even though it is still too early to evaluate in detail the achievements and the limits of the Third Quest, after several decades and hundreds of publications it is clear that there is no agreed-upon vision of the historical figure of Jesus. It is true that a wide consensus exists as to some of the essential facts of his biography—which is not a small achievement—but,

---

[20] Discovered respectively in 1945 and 1947. Cf. J. M. Robinson (ed.), *The Nag Hammadi Library in English*, San Francisco 1990; F. García Martínez (ed.), *The Dead Sea Scrolls Translated: The Qumran Texts in English*, Grand Rapids 1996.

starting from these, quite different images of Christ can be drawn: from the itinerant cynic philosopher largely unconcerned with the end of the world (J. D. Crossan) to the eschatological prophet (E. P. Sanders); from the Jesus who lacks any awareness of his unique role in human history and, naturally, of his divine nature (M. J. Borg) to the Christ compatible with Nicene-Constantinople orthodoxy (N. T. Wright); from the Jesus hardly interested in politics (G. Vermes) to the revolutionary Christ (R. A. Horsley).[21]

This variety of the results shows that, beyond a list of more or less probable facts about his life, it is not possible to reach a "purely scientific" vision of Jesus, free from interpretations of a particular stamp.

The work of John P. Meier, *A Marginal Jew: Rethinking the Historical Jesus*, began to be published at the time in which the Third Quest was reaching its apogee and beginning to enter an impasse. The monumental work of this North American exegete represented an attempt to evaluate with objectivity what can and what cannot be known about Jesus, collecting the immense variety of opinions expressed about this. The five bulky volumes that make it up, written over two decades,[22] begin by proposing the following imaginary experiment:

> Suppose that a Catholic, a Protestant, a Jew and an agnostic—all honest historians cognizant of 1st- century religious movements—were locked up in the bowels of the Harvard Divinity

---

[21] M. J. Borg, *Conflict, Holiness and Politics in the Teachings of Jesus*, New York 1984; M. J. Borg – N. T. Wright, *The Meaning of Jesus: Two Visions*, San Francisco 1999; J. D. Crossan, *The Historical Jesus: The Life of a Mediterranean Jewish Peasant*, San Francisco 1993; R. A. Horsley, *Jesus and the Spiral of Violence: Popular Jewish Resistance in Roman Palestine*, San Francisco 1987; E. P. Sanders, *The Historical Figure of Jesus*, London 1993; G. Vermes, *Jesus, the Jew*, New York 1973; N. T. Wright, *Jesus and the Victory of God*, Minneapolis 1996.

[22] J. P. Meier, *A Marginal Jew: Rethinking the Historical Jesus*, New York 1991–2016.

School library, put on a spartan diet, and not allowed to
emerge until they had hammered out a consensus document
on who Jesus of Nazareth was and what he intended in his
own time and place. An essential requirement for this document would be that it be based on purely historical sources
and arguments.[23]

The fruit of this joint investigation would be to reach a definition of the "historical Jesus"; nevertheless, such a definition
would always be different from the definition of the "real
Jesus." The project to find the historical Jesus, then, is limited
to determining some facts of his life that can be accepted by
all scholars, independently of their beliefs. To achieve this, in
continuity with the procedures of the historical-critical method,
Meier proposes to isolate the facts and sayings of Jesus from
their context in the gospels and to examine whether each of
them can be validated by this interconfessional consensus.

Alasdair MacIntyre has argued that "we cannot . . . characterize behavior independently of intentions, and we cannot
characterize intentions independently of the settings which
make those intentions intelligible both to agents themselves
and to others."[24] According to this Scottish philosopher, "the
concept of an intelligible action is a more fundamental concept
than that of an action as such."[25] In other words, in the case of
human actions, the naked fact—the raw data—is secondary
with respect to the intelligible action, since in order to arrive
at the former it is necessary to eliminate from the action its
inherent intentionality and isolate it from the context that situates it and gives it meaning. For this reason, "narrative history
of a certain kind turns out to be the basic and essential genre
for the characterization of human actions."[26]

[23] Ibid., vol. I, 1.
[24] A. C. MacIntyre, *After Virtue: A Study in Moral Theory*, Notre Dame
IN 2007, 206.
[25] Ibid., 209. Cf. S. Hauerwas, "The Virtues of Alasdair MacIntyre,"
First Things 2007.
[26] A. C. MacIntyre, *After Virtue*, 208.

The thought-experiment of Meier shows the secondary character of the historical Jesus, since each of the scholars locked up in the library has his or her own understanding of Jesus, a way of telling the story of his life that gives him a certain identity. The participants bracket their accounts of Jesus in order to limit themselves to deciding whether certain facts and statements did or did not occur. In this way, the historical Jesus defined by Meier, in addition to being different from the real flesh-and-blood Jesus who walked on the roads of Galilee, is the product of an academic investigation that has its source in the gospel accounts, which are epistemologically closer to the real Jesus.

Having reached this point, no one can deny that Jesus lived with a clear intentionality. In fact, the gospels do not transmit events and statements taken out of context, but situate them in a narrative framework that integrates them into the whole of Christ's mission, which consisted in proclaiming by his entire life—words and deeds—the inbreaking of God's Kingdom into history. This made possible a new communion with an astonishing Father who proclaims his unconditional and definitive reconciliation with humanity. From the beginning Jesus surrounded himself with a group of disciples who tried to incarnate, by their way of life, the new reality of the Kingdom. After Easter, this community realized that the project of Jesus not only had not come to an end with the death of their Master, but in addition received its definitive impulse in the resurrection. For this reason, they continued to add new members and to organize communities as ecosystems favorable to the growth of the seed of the Kingdom.

In this context of personal and social transformation the memory of Jesus was conserved; the gospels were written; the canon established. But what was being undertaken was much more than a process of transmitting information, because believing in Jesus did not merely involve affirming certain truths about him, but in involving one's life in his project. Discipleship means inserting one's own story into the story of a community whose final goal is the Kingdom. It is amazing how well Reimarus understood Christian faith when he entitled his book "The Aims of Jesus and His Disciples." In fact, if the disciple's aims are not in line with those of his Master, Christianity is not possible. On the other hand, not being a Christian means believing that this project is insane or nonsensical; it means affirming that Jesus, in his right mind, could not have had such intentions and, finally, that despite what the gospels say, Jesus was another kind of person.

The Jesus of Dogma

Let us now look at what the Creed says. This story begins much earlier than Reimarus, specifically 300 years after Christ, in the fourth century of our era. The emperor Constantine had begun to show favor to Christianity scarcely a decade earlier; the church, which until then had been a prohibited sect, now enjoyed imperial favor.[27] The emperor, and not the pope, convoked the first ecumenical council at Nicaea in the year 325. A heresy, Arianism, threatened the unity of the church and endangered the project of imperial restoration. Arius claimed that Jesus was an inferior divine being, created by God the Father. Against this Nicaea affirmed, in a language taken not from the Bible but from the Greek philosophical tradition, that Christ is *homoousios tō patri*, of the same divine nature as God the Father.

The Nicene-Constantinopolitan Creed constitutes an expanded version of the Apostle's Creed based on the decisions taken at the councils of Nicaea (325) and Constantinople I (381). It is the confession of faith that most Christians still profess

[27] The Edict of Milan, promulgated by the emperor Constantine in the year 313, established freedom of religion, which brought with it the tolerance of Christianity and the end of the persecutions. Constantine did not only tolerate Christianity; he promoted it in various ways, but without making it the official religion.

today. The section on the second person of the Holy Trinity goes like this (the additions of Nicaea to the Apostles' Creed are in italics):

> I believe in one Lord Jesus Christ, the Only Begotten Son of God, *born of the Father before all ages. God from God, Light from Light, true God from true God, begotten, not made, consubstantial with the Father; through him all things were made. For us men and for our salvation he came down from heaven*, and by the Holy Spirit was incarnate of the Virgin Mary, and became man. For our sake he was crucified under Pontius Pilate, he suffered death and was buried, and rose again on the third day in accordance with the Scriptures. He ascended into heaven and is seated at the right hand of the Father. He will come again in glory to judge the living and the dead and his kingdom will have no end.

The added phrases reflect the principal concern of Nicaea: to affirm the full divinity of Jesus. The words have a rhythm that is practically obsessive: "God from God, Light from Light, true God from true God." It is as if the council fathers were saying: "Is it clear? Jesus is not a minor god—as Arius affirmed—but God with the same divinity as the Creator, 'made of the same stuff,' *consubstantial with the Father*." Only after this insistence does the Creed continue with the incarnation of the Son in the womb of the Virgin, his death on the cross and his resurrection, his ascension into heaven and the final judgment.

The somersault that this formula makes over the earthly life of Christ cannot fail to attract attention: "[he] was incarnate of the Virgin Mary, and became man. For our sake he was crucified under Pontius Pilate." From the incarnation it passes directly to the crucifixion, without saying a single word about what happened between the two events. The life of Jesus, the principal content of the gospels, finds hardly any room in the Creed.

This does not mean that the conciliar fathers considered the Gospel irrelevant. The objective of the Christological councils was to limit certain interpretations of the person of Jesus that were considered unacceptable. In this sense, the Creed represents a frame that limits the ways of interpreting Jesus that the New Testament allows.[28] The problem with the Jesus of dogma arises when it supplants the image of Jesus presented by the gospels: the frame—the Creed—is presented as the work that we have to contemplate, whereas the image, the true work of art—the Gospel—becomes a simple appendage.

According to the New Testament, Jesus is the Son of God. In this sense, dogma is rooted in the Scriptures. But the gospels tell us much more, and this *more* has to do above all with God's way of being. This is especially evident in the synoptic gospels: Jesus shows himself more interested in showing us who the Father is than in telling us who he is himself.[29]

Adolphe Gesché states that "it could well be the case that we have never really taken seriously into consideration the theology, the discourse about God, that appears implicitly in the message of Jesus." According to this Belgian theologian, beginning already in the second century, Christian reflection began to take for granted an idea of God that it received from the Greek philosophers "without assuming the consequences of the transformation of the idea of God that Christ had brought."[30] But the insistence on affirming that Jesus is the Son of God, without letting him tell us *what* God he is Son of, leads to a perversion of his Gospel. The Creed without the Scriptures is incapable of enabling us to critique the idea of God; without the gospels the concept of God remains at the mercy of the

[28] N. T. Wright, "Whence and Whither Historical Jesus Studies in the Life of the Church?," in N. Perrin – R. B. Hays (eds.), *Jesus, Paul and the People of God: A Theological Dialogue with N. T. Wright*, Downers Grove 2011.

[29] "A Christology in which the face of Christ captures all the attention runs important risks." A. Gesché, *Jesucristo (Dios para pensar VI)*, Salamanca 2002, 29. Adolphe Gesché (1928–2003) was one of the most influential European theologians of the late twentieth century. His work is, however, little known in the English-speaking world. His collection of books, *Dieu pour penser*, has been translated into Spanish, Portuguese, Italian and Polish, but not into English. Our translation here is from the Spanish version.

[30] Ibid., 31.

manipulations of the dynamisms of power, present to a greater or lesser degree in all the institutions both inside and outside of the church.[31] In this way, the surprising God of Jesus who is overjoyed to find the lost sheep, who causes his Kingdom to grow with the discretion of a pinch of yeast that a woman mixes into the dough, a Father who forgives without asking for explanations and lets his sun shine on the good and the wicked, a king who invites beggars and cripples to the wedding of his son, remains blurred. Unfortunately, this God of the Gospel, who is expressed eminently in his crucified Christ, has been substituted on many occasions by a "Supreme Being," authoritarian and patriarchal, who in addition is a stern judge.

The Creed was not designed to take the place of the Gospel. The subordinate position of the Creed within the celebration of the Eucharist, as a kind of finishing touch after the gospel reading and the homily, illustrates how this prayer functions as a frame for the principle image, which is Jesus proclaimed in the Gospel.

The Gospel is the image; the Creed is the frame. The Creed confirms that Jesus is the Son of God, and the Gospel proclaims the God Jesus is Son of. It narrates the Good News of a God who loved the world so much that he did not even keep back his beloved Son (Rom 8:32). Across the centuries, for many Christians—including some theologians—the interest in affirming that Jesus is God displaced the central question of the Gospel: the amazement to discover a surprising God, the one who became manifest in the teaching and person of Christ.[32] To recover the correct relationship between the Gospel and the Creed, between the painting and the frame, we have to place the Gospel at the center of our attention.[33]

[31] Cf. A. C. MacIntyre, *After Virtue*, 194–195.

[32] Cf. A. Gesché, *Jesucristo*, 32.

[33] Cf. N. T. Wright, "Whence and Whither Historical Jesus Studies in the Life of the Church?" 130–133.

The Jesus of the Gospels

Let us call "the canonical Jesus" the image of Jesus transmitted in different ways by the documents that make up the canon of the New Testament, especially the four gospels, interpreted critically. If the gospel narratives differ in important details, it is unquestionable that they recount the life of the same man, recognizable in each one of them. The canonical Jesus is not a least common denominator of all the sources, like Meier's historical Jesus, but the three-dimensional image that is formed from them, not exempt from tensions or contradictions. Each one of these testimonies has to be interpreted taking into account its own cultural horizon, applying the critical methods that have been developed in the course of the last two centuries.

To manage to understand precisely this Jesus of the canon, the Jesus of the gospels, we have to situate him in the context of the tradition within which the gospels came into being and within which was formed the canon that recognized them as a revelation from God. During the last few years, studies on the gospels have accorded growing importance to the role of *oral tradition*.[34] If we realize that the written gospels arose in the second Christian generation, in other words beginning around the year 70, the decisive role of oral tradition becomes evident. It kept alive the memory of Christ during the forty years that elapsed between his death and the composition of

---

[34] Cf. P. J. Achtemeier, "*Omne verbum sonat*: The New Testament and the Oral Environment of Late Western Antiquity," *Journal of Biblical Literature* 109 (1990); T. E. Boomershine, "Jesus of Nazareth and the Watershed of Ancient Orality and Literacy," *Semeia* 65 (1994); R. C. Culley, "Oral Tradition and Biblical Studies," *Oral Tradition* 1 (1986); J. Dewey, "Oral Methods of Structuring Narrative in Mark," *Interpretation* 43 (1989); id., "The Gospel of Mark as an Oral-aural Event: Implications of Interpretation," in E. V. McKnight – E. S. Malbon (eds.), *The New Literary Criticism and the New Testament*, Valley Forge 1994; J. D. G. Dunn, *Jesus Remembered*, Grand Rapids 2003; A. de Mingo Kaminouchi, *But It Is Not So Among You: Echoes of Power in Mark 10:32–45*, London 2003, 42–72.

the first gospel. It is clear, moreover, that oral tradition did not cease as soon as the first written sources were composed. At the beginning of the second century, decades after the composition of the last canonical gospel, a Christian named Papias wrote these words:

> But if I met with any one who had been a follower of the elders any where, I made it a point to inquire what were the declarations of the elders. What was said by Andrew, Peter or Philip. What by Thomas, James, John, Matthew, or any other of the disciples of our Lord. What was said by Aristion, and the presbyter John, disciples of the Lord; *for I do not think that I derived so much benefit from books as from the living voice of those that are still surviving.*[35]

I want to emphasize here a certain disdain expressed concerning "books" and the greater respect that, for this believer, "the living voice" merits. Those books are nothing less than the gospels! And so, at the beginning of the second century, despite the prestige that the written gospels had acquired, oral tradition received an even greater reverence, at least from some Christians.

The role of oral tradition, as a bridge to connect the real Jesus who preached in Galilee with the images of Jesus transmitted by the gospels, remains indisputable. But why should we limit ourselves to speaking of "oral tradition"? Why not just speak of "tradition"? The substitution of "tradition" for "oral tradition" responds to a focus on the materiality of the words, proper to fundamentalistic Protestantism. According to this vision, that applies in an extremely literal way the Lutheran principle of *sola scriptura*, tradition disappeared after the composition of the gospels.[36] According to this way of

[35] Eusebius of Caesarea, *The Ecclesiastical History*, III, 39, 4; my italics.
[36] This ultraconservative interpretation of the principle of *sola scriptura* is not shared by most of the Protestant churches, as is shown by the conclusions of the Fourth Conference of Faith and Order celebrated by

understanding revelation, the function of *tradition* was to be *oral tradition*; in other words, it was the means of keeping the Word alive during those decades of fragility when Scripture did not exist. And since the only reason for tradition was to produce Scripture, once this was composed, it ceased to exist.

The Catholic Church has always insisted that this tradition did not disappear with the appearance of Scripture, but that it remained, and still remains, alive alongside it. Revelation requires both, Scripture and Tradition, which should not be understood as two separate channels, each with its own content of truths, as the preconciliar schema *De fontibus revelationis* claimed. On the contrary, according to the constitution *Dei Verbum*, Tradition and Scripture flow "from the same divine well-spring, both of them merge, in a sense, and move towards the same goal" (DV 9).

Yves Congar taught us that Tradition is *another means* required by revelation for its very nature, because there is something that no scripture—however sacred it might be—can transmit, above all if we understand revelation not as the communication of a collection of information about the deity, but as the personal revelation of God himself. This revelation cannot be

---

the World Council of Churches in Montreal in 1963 and which says in its section II, 45: "In our present situation, we wish to reconsider the problem of Scripture and Tradition, or rather that of Tradition and Scripture. And therefore we wish to propose the following statement as a fruitful way of reformulating the question. Our starting-point is that we are all living in a tradition which goes back to our Lord and has its roots in the Old Testament, and are all indebted to that tradition inasmuch as we have received the revealed truth, the Gospel, through its being transmitted from one generation to another. Thus we can say that we exist as Christians by the Tradition of the Gospel (the *paradosis* of the *kerygma*) testified in Scripture, transmitted in and by the Church through the power of the Holy Spirit." Cf. R. Schutz – M. Thurian, *Revelation, a Protestant View; the Dogmatic Constitution on Divine Revelation, a Commentary*, Westminster MD 1968, 28–40. The minutes of the Fourth World Conference on Faith and Order, Montréal 1963, can be consulted at https://archive.org/stream/wccfops2.046/wccfops2.046_djvu.txt.

adequately expressed by a text alone; it requires another means provided by tradition. Congar wrote:

> Tradition . . . is the communication of the entire heritage of the apostles, effected in a different way from that of their writings. We must try to define it more precisely and describe the original way in which it was done. It was not by discursive means, with all the accurate and precise formulation that this allows; it was by means of the concrete experience of life and of the familiar everyday realities of existence. It could well be compared to all that is implied by the idea of upbringing as opposed to instruction.[37]

The Christians of the first generation, responsible for the crucial function of keeping alive the memory of Christ through oral tradition, did not consider that their mission consisted basically in preserving the words and acts of Jesus. These believers were involved in a form of life that impelled them to be witnesses to the Kingdom of God. Conserving and handing down the memories of their Teacher was an important practice, but they were part of an ecosystem of other practices also essential for their existence: hospitality offered to itinerant missionaries, community meetings that included singing and prophecy, the celebration of the Lord's Supper, different forms of mutual aid and solidarity, non-violent resistance to persecution, the diversity of ministries in order to ensure a flourishing community life, and so on.[38]

The gospels are not a simple collection of elements of oral information cleverly put together; they arose from the narrative traditions that nourished the life of the Christian communities where they were written. The vitality of these churches was sustained by an ecosystem of practices that incarnated the new relationship with God, and among human

[37] Y. Congar, *The Meaning of Tradition*, San Francisco 2004, 22.
[38] Cf. W. A. Meeks, *The Moral World of the First Christians*, Philadelphia 1986; F. Rivas, *La vida cotidiana de los primeros cristianos*, Estella 2011.

beings, that made the hope of the Kingdom possible. As Christians we read the gospels in the context of this living Tradition, not just as texts containing interesting information about Jesus, but as treasured documents of a community that found in them the expression of images of Christ that are essential in order to enter into relation with his being.

In the bosom of this tradition dogma also arose, the function of which is not to replace the Gospel, but to orient its reading and to exclude possible interpretations of Jesus that contradict the tradition believed in and lived by the church. But here lies the danger of the sclerosis of dogma. An obsessive affirmation of certain "formulas of faith" can replace living access to the Christ of whom the gospels speak. In this sense, the historical quest of Jesus—including that undertaken with anti-ecclesial intentions—has represented and still represents a salutary lesson to "awaken us from our dogmatic slumber" and fix our eyes on Jesus, that first-century Jew in whose humanity Christians confess the definitive revelation of God.

Disciples of Jesus

The public life of Christ was centered on the proclamation of the Kingdom of God. The Synoptic Gospels present him in this way. Let us begin with the shortest and probably the oldest of the three, Mark.

The good news of "Jesus Christ, Son of God" (Mark 1:1) begins with a quote from Isaiah that speaks of a "voice crying in the wilderness: prepare the way of the Lord!"[39] Fulfilling the prophecy, John the Baptist appears, preaching and baptizing. In this way, Mark situates the biography of Jesus in the horizon of the hopes of liberation of the people of Israel.[40] The

---

[39] In reality, Mark 1:2–3 is a combination of Exod 23:20, Isa 40:3 and Mal 3:1.

[40] The gospels are, in this sense, biographies. Not in the modern sense, but in the way such books were written in Antiquity, with the specific

wilderness evokes in the Bible the Exodus, the flight of Israel from slavery in Egypt. Just as the Israelites crossed the Jordan River to enter the Promised Land, John prepares those who flock to him for a definitive intervention of God, which will radically transform their lives and bring to birth a new world. According to Mark's account, Jesus enters history in a specific context: his coming is linked to the fulfillment of the prophecy made to Isaiah and with the purpose of bringing the people of God back from its long exile.[41] The arrest of the Baptist is that signal that the time has finally come: "After John was arrested, Jesus came to Galilee proclaiming the Good News (*euangelion*) of God. He said, 'The time has come and the Kingdom of God is at hand,[42] change your hearts and believe in the Good News'" (1:15).

In the following chapters, Mark shows the reader how Jesus inaugurates the Kingdom of God on earth or, in other words, what the world would be like if God really began to take charge of things. His reply is: the sick would be healed, those possessed by evil spirits would recover their sanity, sinners would be forgiven. According to the evangelist, Jesus announced his message of salvation to all, but he came especially to those wounded by life and to the outcasts of society, to invite them into the Kingdom. From the beginning until the end of his public ministry, he was surrounded by a community of disciples, men and women (cf. 1:16-20; 15:40-41). Among them he chose twelve, in this way re-establishing symbolically the

---

character traits of a person like Jesus. Cf. S. Guijarro, *Los cuatro evangelios*, Salamanca 2010, 57–60.

[41] Tom Wright argues, in my opinion correctly, that some Jews of the time of Jesus felt that the nation's exile in Babylonia did not come to an end with the rebuilding of Jerusalem and its temple in the fifth century BCE. The promises of Second Isaiah had still to be realized fully by a divine intervention. Cf. N. T. Wright, *The New Testament and the People of God: Christian Origins and the Question of God* I, Minneapolis 1996, 268–272.

[42] The Greek expression "*ēngiken hē basileia tou theou*" literally means "the Kingdom of God has approached," in other words, the Kingdom "is arriving, is already at hand."

tribes of Israel, sign of the inauguration of the Kingdom (cf. 3:13-19; Isa 49:6). The two miracles of the multiplication of the loaves (cf. 6:30-44 and 8:1-10) realize another of the prophecies concerning the Messiah and God's Reign—the messianic banquet. "The Lord of hosts is providing on this mountain, for all peoples, a feast of rich foods and choice wine" (Isa 25:6). Is the long-awaited Kingdom of God finally arriving? This is undoubtedly what the disciples as well as the crowds were asking themselves.

And it is precisely at this moment, in the midst of Mark's narrative, that Jesus asks, "Who do you say that I am?" Peter replies, "You are the Christ" (8:29). We are at the crux of the narration. At this point the argument takes a brusque turn: Jesus tells his disciples that the Son of Man will have to suffer greatly, be rejected, die and rise (8:31-32). The triumphal crescendo that had characterized the revelation of the Kingdom in the first eight chapters is replaced by the journey up to Jerusalem, a hard road of discipleship that will reveal a Messiah who is going to die on the cross. This radical turn of events does not mean, however, that Christ's mission has changed; his death and resurrection will inaugurate definitively the Kingdom of God. Over the cross, a notice, despite having been written in mockery, testifies to the truth about the Crucified One: "The King of the Jews" (15:26).

Jesus had said, "Whoever wants to be great among you will be your servant, and whoever wants to be first will be the slave of all. For the Son of Man did not come to be served but to serve, and to give his life as a ransom for the many" (10:43-45). The Kingdom that Jesus comes to inaugurate will not be imposed by violence or power, but through humble service and the gift of his life. God never forces anyone. Christ witnesses to this non-violent God by his life and his death.

This basic argument traced out by Mark is picked up by the evangelists Matthew and Luke. Their gospels can be considered as "revised and augmented editions" of Mark, the first gospel. Both add to the succinct story of their predecessor the gospels of infancy and the appearances of the Risen Christ.

Both introduce many sayings of Jesus that very probably come from a document that is now lost, "the source of sayings Q."[43] Nonetheless, each one presents its own perspective. Matthew, writing for a Jewish-Christian community, describes Jesus as a new Moses who comes as founder of a new Israel; Luke, who aims his gospel at Christians coming from the pagan world, characterizes Jesus as a Teacher who invites people to mercy and to sharing. But for both, Jesus is basically the same person as he is for Mark: the one who comes to announce the Kingdom and to inaugurate it by his life, death and resurrection.

The way the evangelist John narrates the story of Jesus is very different from the other three. From the beginning, the Fourth Gospel presents Jesus as "the Word of God made flesh" (1:14). After his baptism and the calling of the first disciples, the action begins at the wedding of Cana in Galilee (2:1-12). This is the first of the seven signs (*semeia*) that are presented in the first half of this gospel; each one of them shows symbolically that Jesus is the one sent from God who comes to make a new access to the Father possible. The second part begins with the narrative of the Last Supper: Jesus kneels before his disciples to wash their feet (13:1-20). In this way, John uses acts to express what Mark said in words: "I have come not to be served, but to serve." After long discourses of Christ on the night of his farewell, John tells the story of his Passion. And like the synoptics, he refers to the inscription that Pilate had placed on the cross: "The King of the Jews" (19:19). Finally, he narrates the encounters of Mary Magdalene, Peter and the other disciples with the Risen Christ. Although John, unlike the synoptics, almost never uses the expression "the Kingdom of God" (only in 3:3-5 and 18:36), Jesus remains the One sent from God who comes to inaugurate a new closeness to God not by force, but through service and martyrdom.

The Christian communities that wrote the gospels saw themselves as immersed in the process of transformation set

---

[43] Cf. S. Guijarro, *Los dichos de Jesús: Introducción al Documento Q*, Salamanca 2014.

in motion by Jesus, the inaugurator of the Kingdom. The revolution begun by Christ did not stop with his death, because he rose from the dead. They also experienced a new presence of God, which they called *to pneuma hagion*, "Holy Spirit," that impelled them to undertake a new mission. Inspired by the Spirit, they came together often to give thanks for their new life and, when they repeated the same gestures and words of Jesus at the Last Supper, they felt the Lord present in the midst of the community (1 Cor 11:17-34). These early Christians shared much more than a few ideas or some memories of the Master; they had in common their trust in Christ and mutual love, as well as facing together the risks and the sufferings of persecution.

The four canonical gospels reflect the faith of those early Christians. In their pages we do not merely find a list of biographical data, but a narrative that present the acts and sayings of Jesus inserted in a story line that reveals a global meaning. It expresses the interpretation that the first Christian community made of the person of Jesus. It constitutes, therefore, a *particular* vision concerning who Jesus was, but this interpretation is linked to the *real* Jesus in that which was for him the essential: the goal of his existence; in fact, nothing helps us to understand a person better than knowing the meaning he gives to his life.[44] For Jesus, to proclaim God's closeness, with whom he felt intimately united, and to announce to everyone, particularly those outcast and excluded, the invitation to participate in his Kingdom was the reason for his life. With his actions he tried to manifest the inbreaking of this Reign into human history, and out of faithfulness to this he gave his life.

The key to Christianity is whether we give credit or not to what the disciples affirm in the gospels: that Jesus was risen and that his project to bring God's Kingdom to earth had only begun. Along with countless Christians throughout history,

---

[44] "The Aims of Jesus" is the title and the content of one of the groundbreaking books of the Third Quest: B. Meyer, *The Aims of Jesus*, London 1979.

they made this Kingdom their reason for living. The precise terms they used for it are not important: Saint Paul, scarcely two decades after Christ, hardly ever uses the expression "the Kingdom of God." The important thing is that, starting from Christ, God begins to enter human history in a manner beyond all our hopes. He sent his Spirit, who acted and keeps acting until the Kingdom will finally culminate in "a new heaven and a new earth," where justice shines forth and every tear will be wiped away (Rev 21:1-3).

The first Christians felt they were privileged to have been chosen by God for a unique adventure:[45] to be protagonists of the definitive transformation of reality, a process already underway ever since the man Jesus achieved what seemed restricted to a fantasy world: to leap over that wall that rises up at the end of every human being's life—death. Those men and women believed not only that Christ was risen, but in addition that what took place in him was going to occur also in them, because Jesus was the first-fruits of a new humanity to which they hoped to belong. Some, like Paul, even thought they would not experience death before seeing the arrival in fullness of the Kingdom of God (1 Thess 4:15).

As we know well, the end did not come immediately, but this did not prevent the expansion of the Christian faith. The "When?" was not the important thing, but rather the "What?" and the "How?" The Kingdom had already been inaugurated by the death and resurrection of Christ, and the Spirit of God was acting effectively in the world. Those men and women, often persecuted and subject to trials, did not always find it easy to recognize that God was on their side and that the Kingdom was beginning to sprout and silently transform reality. It was not always evident to their sight, but they had faith. Jesus had told them that the power of God is not like that of earthly

---

[45] Cf. S. Hauerwas, "Christianity: It's Not a Religion, It's an Adventure" (1991), in J. Berkman – M. Cartwright (eds.), *The Hauerwas Reader*, Durham NC 2001.

governors, that God's strength acts without imposing itself on anyone. The first communities understood that being a Christian means witnessing to this God and putting themselves at the service of his Reign, in the hope that humanity and "creation itself will be liberated from slavery to corruption and enter into the glorious freedom of the children of God" (Rom 8:21).

This is not the place even to try to sum up everything that happened afterwards. It is clear that the itineraries followed by different Christian communities in the course of two thousand years of existence cannot be simplified in a few pages. What we can affirm here is that what we call "Christianity" has no meaning if it is detached from a concrete community that accepts responsibility for the Kingdom as a project that is not only religious, but also ethical in all the aspects of human life—in family, culture, politics and economics. Following the witness of the first communities, it is clear that Christianity cannot simply be understood as a "religious motivation" added to a life already configured by other intentions.

The Body of Christ, Locus of Revelation

Christian ethics is at the service of the transformation of reality that started out through the inbreaking of the Kingdom of God through the ministry of Jesus. *Revelation* is the name that Christians gave to this approach of God in Jesus to the world, which changed everything. It is true that the Spirit blows where it will (John 3:8), inside and outside of the church, but for some reason God wished there to be a community that cultivated the Kingdom intentionally. God counts on men and women who commit their lives to be configured by the story of Jesus.

> Being Christian is a way of life; it's being part of God's story. To be Christian is to appreciate what God has done for us through Jesus of Nazareth. Being Christian doesn't mean following a set of rules or principles; Christianity depends

on the character of people's lives. The Gospel has no meaning unless it can be lived out and *embodied* in people's lives.[46]

Embodied: that is the key. "The *Logos* became *flesh*," says John
in the prologue of his gospel (John 1:14). This affirmation is
what distinguishes Christian revelation from other theological
or philosophical visions of the world. In the person of Jesus it
is possible to encounter God in the flesh, that soft fabric that
covers our bones and is a symbol of human frailty. "Christianity is the most bodily of religions,"[47] said Timothy Radcliffe,
speaking of the Eucharist. *Caro salutis cardo* ("the flesh is the
hinge of salvation") wrote Tertullian, a Christian of the second
century. The transformation of life produced by the Gospel
affects our entire being, including the intelligence, but its hinge
is not the mind; it is that *concrete self* that Paul of Tarsus calls
"the body."

At the center of our faith, then, is the Body of Christ, born
of the Virgin Mary, which passed through the same stages as
every human being from its conception: it was formed in the
womb of a mother, came into the world through birth, suckled
the breasts of Mary and learned a language, a culture and a
trade. Jesus passed through childhood and adolescence, was
baptized in the Jordan, fasted, ate with tax-collectors and sinners, and finally, before departing, said a few words over a loaf
of bread and entrusted it to his disciples as a sign of the Passion
that was going to destroy him, "This is my body." This body,
with its history and its wounds, is the reality that Christians
affirm has risen from the dead, thus realizing in this concrete
location in our world the fullness of the Kingdom. Origen, the
great theologian of the third century, said that Jesus is the
autobasileia, the Kingdom realized in a human being.[48]

---

[46] Ibid., 522. Italics mine.

[47] T. Radcliffe, *Afectividad y eucaristia*, talk given at the XXXIV Days of
Vocational Youth Ministry, Madrid, October 8–10, 2004.

[48] In Greek, *basileia* means "kingdom" and *autobasileia*, the Kingdom
contained in a person, Christ. Cf. Origen, *Spirit and Fire: A Thematic An-
thology of His Writings*, Edinburgh 2001, 362.

Christ is the Word made *flesh*, human vulnerability, in whom God himself embraces our weakness. This flesh is also the locus of a deep communion with others. The Holy Spirit comes to touch this soft and tender reality that we are most deeply and that we often try to protect with the armor of our masks and apparent identities. In this place we can open ourselves, disarmed, to those who suffer impoverishment and oppression, to those in need: "Whatever you did to one of these, the least of my brothers and sisters, you did for me" (Matt 25:40). The Word born in flesh invites us to divest ourselves of all that makes us insensible to them; we are called to "remove the armor, the hard carapace, the iron glove that would prevent our humanity being touched."[49]

The first Christians understood themselves as a community that made the Body of Christ incarnate on the earth, offering in his name a space of hospitality and communion. This communion does not consist above all in an agreement concerning common ideals or shared doctrine, but takes place on a more bodily level. Sharing bread, singing together, removing our clothes to receive baptism, fasting, laying on hands, etc., are actions that transform what we are through practices that involve our entire being. It is a process that begins as a gift discovered with astonishment, but that goes forward by taking into account as well the cooperation of our will, our efforts and our work.

Christian ethics is at the service of this transformation as a reflection that helps us to understand the way in which the different practices that make up the Christian life are articulated, ordered to configure the community and each believer in the image of Christ. The community that we call the church does not have its purpose in itself; it exists to be a sign and instrument of fraternity for the entire human family. Christian ethics has to show concrete paths to realize this mission in a

---

[49] T. Radcliffe, *Take the Plunge: Living Baptism and Confirmation*, London 2012, 162.

world that already is undergoing the birth pangs of a new age (Rom 8:22).

We now have to find a conceptual scheme that enables us to explain in words the grammar of this transformation. This will be the subject of the next chapter. We will propose the *ethics of virtues* as the framework of concepts that will enable us to express what happens in Christian life when "faith acts through love" (Gal 5:6).

CHAPTER THREE

A Grammar of Ethics

Christian ethics is at the service of the changes that take place when the God of Jesus Christ becomes present in our lives. With the passing of time and the support of our collaboration, the Holy Spirit configures us to the image of Jesus. As we pointed out in the previous chapter, this transformation does not occur only on an emotional or intellectual level; it has its center of gravity in the body.

Modern neuroscience uses the expression "neuroplasticity" to refer to an intrinsic property of the human brain, which consists in the ability to modify the synaptic connections between the neurons, to make new habits possible in response to new needs.[1] This capacity of the brain to change its hardwiring and acquire new skills is only the most extreme case of the "open architecture" with which the human body is designed. The members of our species are not limited to one type of food; our taste can be educated so that we even find raw fish or moldy cheese tasty. Our sexual desire is not limited to fertile periods like most animals, nor are our courtship rituals fixed once and for all. Our hands can be taught to play a violin or to pilot a space shuttle. Our muscles can be trained to accomplish gymnastic feats or to break speed and endurance records

[1] A. Pascual-Leone – A. Amedi – F. Fregni – L. B. Merabet, "The Plastic Human Brain Cortex," *Annual Review of Neuroscience* 28 (2005).

that seemed unbeatable, but they can also atrophy on a sofa. We human beings are open systems that can channel our possibilities in different directions and reach our true potential only by training and exercise.

We are social beings as well. We are born more destitute than any other animal. We need to receive the exquisite care of a mother to survive and develop our most fundamental abilities. Our most basic social capacity, communicating through language, is acquired through contact with other people who, from infancy, take us seriously enough to speak to us. Our period of immaturity is the longest of any animal species, and in complex societies like ours the period of formation extends beyond physical maturity. Even as adults we cannot enjoy a full life alone: we require a vast social network that interacts with us.

These two ideas, the need for training as well as social relations so that human potential can reach fullness, were at the basis of the moral tradition that originated with Aristotle (384–322 BCE) and is called "virtue ethics." This current of moral thought has as its central category not law, but virtue. We call "virtue" a capacity, developed through learning and exercise in social contexts, that forms part of the character of a person, of what he or she is.

The Surprising Return to Aristotle

Since the last quarter of the twentieth century we have seen, in the realm of philosophy and of Christian theology, a growing interest in virtue ethics.[2] In addition, in the more special-

---

[2] According to a bibliographical study published in 1997, virtue ethics took first place among the interests of moral theologians in the United States. Cf. H. Schlögel, "Tugend – Kasuistik – Biographie: Trends und ökumenische Perspektiven in der Moraltheologie der USA," *Catholica* 51 (1997). Since then, this tendency has been confirmed in the English-speaking world as well as in other linguistic areas. Cf., for example, M. Vidal, "¿Es posible actualizar, de forma inteligente e innovadora, la 'ética

ized field of New Testament ethics, in recent years a number of works have appeared that show the possibilities of this focus.[3]

In the first chapter, we pointed out that the Council of Trent (1545–1563) had fostered the adoption of the casuistic paradigm in Catholic morality. This approach was centered on the law and its application to concrete cases. Two centuries after this council, and independently of it, a secular moral philosophy began to develop in Europe whose goal was to find a basis for ethics within the limits of pure reason. Certain philosophers, notably David Hume (1711–1776) and Immanuel Kant (1724–1804), tried to establish the legitimacy of moral laws in purely rational terms, independent of any arguments based on Christian revelation.

At the origins of this project we find the great military conflicts that devastated Europe during the sixteenth and seventeenth centuries. The most serious was the Thirty Years' War, which began when the Protestant nobility of Bohemia rebelled against the Catholic emperor Ferdinand II in an episode known as the Second Defenestration of Prague (1618). The conflict spread to all of central Europe, fanned by the hatred that erupted between the different Christian confessions and by the ambition of the rulers to increase their power. The result was the bloodiest war that the continent had ever known. Some regions lost half of their population through both direct casualties and the famines and epidemics caused by the violence.

---

de la virtud'?" *Moralia* 27 (2004) 382–390; M. Martinez Mauri, "Perspectivas actuales sobre la virtud: Estudio bibliográfico," *Pensamiento* 48 (1992), and the bibliography that the review *Moralia* publishes each year.

[3] D. S. Cunningham, *Christian Ethics: The End of the Law*, London 2008; D. J. Harrington – J. F. Keenan, *Jesus and Virtue Ethics: Building Bridges between New Testament Studies and Moral Theology*, Lanham 2002; N. T. Wright, *Virtue Reborn*, London 2010. The work of W. C. Spohn, *Go and Do Likewise: Jesus and Ethics*, New York 1999, can be considered groundbreaking in the dialogue between virtue ethics and New Testament studies in Catholic morality.

After the signing of the peace treaty of Westphalia (1648), a new basis had to be found for coexistence. It was evident, at any rate, that the ideal of a Europe united under a common Christian heritage had been buried on the battlefields. Some of the most brilliant thinkers of Europe launched the project to establish ethics and politics on a more secure basis than that of a revelation, the different interpretations of which had caused so much misfortune. Their aspiration was that reason could dawn in a Europe over which religious fanaticism had cast a shadow.[4]

The thinkers of the Enlightenment affirmed that it was possible to justify the morality of acts, both in the private and in the public spheres, without any reference to a transcendent end. This silence about ends and the turning away from medieval Christian morality characterized the ethical project of the Enlightenment in its different variations. Thinkers as distinct as Kant, Hume and Locke agreed in defining the object of moral reflection as the act and not the actor. In this way, a curious coincidence occurred: both in its Catholic and its secular versions, Western ethics of the last centuries centered its attention on the study of norms. As a result, when we speak of ethics today, people tacitly assume that we are referring to laws and obligations, to decisions we have to take, especially in difficult circumstances.

We are so accustomed to the fact that ethics deals with laws and obligations that it may surprise us to discover that, at the beginning of the Western philosophical tradition, morality had little to do with norms or specific cases. Its task was quite different. For Aristotle, the author of the first treatises on ethics in our cultural tradition—*Nichomachean Ethics* and *Eudemian Ethics*[5]—the purpose of moral philosophy is to help people to

---

[4] Cf. R. Gascoigne, *The Public Forum and Christian Ethics*, Cambridge 2008, 30–31.

[5] There is a third work of ethics whose attribution to Aristotle is disputed: *Magna Moralia*.

attain happiness by means of a virtuous life. The word "law" (*nomos*) almost never appears in these works and, when it does, it refers to civil law and not moral norms. In these treatises, Aristotle almost never discusses cases of conscience or decisions; his interest lies not in isolated acts taken out of context, but in the habitual activities that form the character of a person. The basic concepts that structure his reflection are happiness, virtue and friendship.

In the last few decades we have seen a waning of that era of civilization that we call the modern age, and more and more authors are turning their eyes to the moral tradition that had been marginalized with the emergence of Enlightenment thought. At the beginning of this "return to virtue" we find the critical and groundbreaking thought of Alasdair MacIntyre. His work, *After Virtue*, published in 1981, constitutes a frontal attack on the philosophical project of the Enlightenment.[6] After showing the incoherence of the different ethical systems that have proliferated in the Western world from the beginnings of the modern era until today, MacIntyre proposes a return to the thought of Aristotle and to his virtue ethics as the only way out of the situation of moral chaos that, in his opinion, characterizes our time.

According to MacIntyre's analysis, the different philosophical schools of the Enlightenment, although differing greatly among themselves, all assume as their project the rational justification of moral norms. According to this program, ethics should be concerned with regulating actions by means of laws, while bracketing the intentions and aims with which people operate. MacIntyre criticizes this approach, arguing that, in the final analysis, what makes a human act intelligible is its

---

[6] MacIntyre was born in Glasgow (Scotland) in 1929, although he spent most of his academic career in the United States, ending up at the University of Notre Dame (Indiana). He is the author of many books, but is known primarily for the one mentioned here: *After Virtue: A Study in Moral Theory*, Notre Dame 1981. The second and third editions (1984 and 2007) retain the same text, while adding respectively an epilogue and a new prologue.

purpose; in fact, we cannot have a rational conversation about ethics if we exclude the theme of the aims of the actions.

The ethical systems of modernity are centered on the law—which has to be equal for everyone—and try to resolve the morality of actions independently of the person who accomplishes them and the reason why he or she does so. In this way a dichotomy is established between intentionality and content that, according to MacIntyre, makes the moral act unintelligible, because if we do not understand why a person does what he or she does, we will never exactly understand the person's behavior. We can only understand the purpose of an act when it is considered within the horizon of the aim that the person who accomplishes it gives to his or her life as a whole. The axiom that MacIntyre defends is one that Aristotle already expressed in his day: acts have a moral import to the extent to which they are oriented to the aims of human life. We can only understand a moral act when we grasp its meaning, but to understand the meaning of an act we have to situate it within the horizon of the destination towards which the person who accomplished it orients his or her existence.

It is clear that nowadays not everyone believes that his or her life has a transcendent meaning. By "transcendent" we do not necessarily mean "religious"; it would be enough to give it the meaning that Aristotle—who was not a particularly spiritual man—gave to his idea of "the good." By "transcendent" we mean, at least, something that points towards a common good that goes beyond the transient desires of the individual. For many people, life today has no other meaning than to accumulate material possessions and pleasurable experiences. Aristotle would not have hesitated in calling this way of thinking and acting irrational. The Aristotelian moral tradition considers that people act rationally when they orient their lives to a good shared in common with other human beings. In other words, a rational ethical dialogue is possible only among persons who believe that human life has a meaning that goes beyond the whims of each individual.

MacIntyre argues that what remains as a consensus on the legitimacy of moral norms in our culture is only the last bastion of a civilization in ruins. But such a consensus can be sustained only if, in the long run, a rational dialogue concerning the aims of human life can be recovered and if we begin once again a discussion about the content of the common good in our societies. According to MacIntyre, liberal culture, by remaining silent about the purpose and the destination of human life, creates a moral and intellectual vacuum that is at the root of the inability to reach rational agreements regarding ethical problems. He states dramatically that to find a way out of the present crisis only two possibilities remain: to slide towards the nihilism of Nietszche, or to return to a teleological ethics like that of Aristotle.

Aristotelian Ethics in Three Words

Eudaimonia

In agreement with Aristotle, both ethics and the rest of human activities are accomplished for an end. Let us allow him to say this in his own words:

> Every art and every inquiry, and similarly every action (*praxis*) and pursuit, is thought to aim at some good . . . the end (*telos*) of the medical art is health, that of shipbuilding a vessel, that of strategy victory, that of economics wealth. (*Nicomachean Ethics*, Book I, 1 [1094a, 1–2, 8–10])[7]

Each activity receives its meaning from an end, and all the activities taken together must converge towards an ultimate end. Otherwise, "the process would go on to infinity, so that our desire would be empty and vain" (ibid. I, 2 [1094a, 21–22]).

---

[7] The quotations from Aristotle are taken from *The Internet Classics Archive*, translated by W. D. Ross, http://classics.mit.edu/Aristotle /nicomachaen.1.i.html, indicating in square brackets the numbers of Bekker.

Human life can only have meaning if it heads towards an end. Aristotle calls this end *happiness*; in the original Greek, *eudaimonia* (ibid. I, 4 [1095a]). *Eudaimonia* and its corresponding adjective *eudaimon* (happy) come from the prefix *eu-*, "good," and the noun *daimōn*, "spirit." It means literally "having a good guardian spirit," in other words, enjoying a life that benefits from the favor of the gods.[8]

In classical Greek, *eudaimonia* was not a technical term; it belonged to the language of the street. Aristotle preferred to reflect on a word used by the people instead of coining a neologism. This choice was born of his conviction that people generally have a certain intuition concerning what happiness is. It is clear that this "vulgar" idea of happiness needs to be purified by philosophical reflection, but it serves as a starting point to connect thought with experience. I think, therefore, that the most adequate translation of *eudaimonia* is "happiness," a term that is still part of everyday usage and about which we all have some notion. But, as was true in the Greece of Aristotle, our conceptions of happiness need to be looked at critically.

Contemporary society tends to conceive happiness as a positive emotional state or as the enjoyment of pleasurable experiences. In fact, for most people being happy means *feeling* happy. According to this way of thinking, happiness is something fragile, almost ephemeral, because it is subject to the capriciousness of the feelings. The happiness that Aristotle speaks about is, on the contrary, a personal and objective achievement, not a passing emotional state. It is an objective that can be reached by means of training and exercise. In this sense, an alternative translation of *eudaimonia* could be "well-being," since it describes a personal and social state that is more objective and stable.[9]

---

[8] C. C. W. Taylor, "Eudaimonia," in E. Craig (ed.), *Routledge Encyclopedia of Philosophy* III, London 1998, 450–452.

[9] The word "well-being" is closer to the Aristotelian *eudaimonia*. The term "happiness," however, has the undoubted advantage of being, like

As already was the case for Aristotle, today as well the definition of the concept of "happiness" remains problematic. The Greek philosopher indicates clearly what happiness is not, refusing emphatically to identify it with the enjoyment of pleasure or the possession of wealth or honor. Without sharing the suspicion of pleasure that characterized the sensibilities of later times, Aristotle recognized that happiness is a reality of another order, because pleasure is inevitably something outside the subject. In addition, he excludes as false—obviously for the same reason—ideals of happiness based on money or prestige. Honor, pleasure and riches are things external to the person; the happiness that he advocates is, by contrast, something inward that belongs to what a person is. For this philosopher, to be happy means to become a certain type of person, to reach a form of being that does justice to what human potential contains.

Aretē

Aristotle, so clear and emphatic when he tells us what happiness is not, shows himself much more cautious when it comes to tracing a profile of the happy man. In any case, despite not defining it with precise characteristics, he is certain that he knows the road leading to happiness—the cultivation of virtue (in Greek, *aretē*). Virtue is a quality or facet of the person that we acquire by training and exercise. We human beings are not born virtuous, but we can become so by exercise. With great pedagogical sense—the *Nicomachean Ethics* was conceived as a book of moral formation dedicated to his son— Aristotle insists that we walk along the road to happiness by accomplishing practices that make us virtuous:

---

eudaimonia in classical Greek, a more common and popular word. Cf. L. J. Jost, "Introduction," in R. A. Shiner – L. J. Jost (eds.), *Eudaimonia and Well-Being: Ancient and Modern Conceptions*, Kelowna 2003, xxii.

> The virtues we get by first exercising them, as also happens
> in the case of the arts as well. For the things we have to learn
> before we can do them, we learn by doing them, e.g. men
> become builders by building and lyreplayers by playing the
> lyre; so too we become just by doing just acts, temperate by
> doing temperate acts, brave by doing brave acts. (*Nicoma-
> chean Ethics*, II, 1 [1103a 31 – 11-3b, 2])

It is important to point out here that Aristotle, like the other
thinkers of Antiquity, understood philosophy not as the exposition of a system of ideas, but as a way of life. He considered
the director of a philosophical school as a spiritual master who
works with each student to lead him along the way of the
"good life." The philosophical works of Antiquity were "written not so much to inform the reader of a doctrinal content but
to form him, to make him traverse a certain itinerary in the
course of which he will make spiritual progress. . . . One must
always approach a philosophical work of antiquity with this
idea of spiritual progress in mind."[10]

In our culture, we tend to understand ethics as a philosophical discipline that helps us to make difficult decisions in complicated situations. What rule of conduct should I apply in this
situation? Is this or that behavior ethical? In this way of thinking, morality appears as knowledge that helps me in times of
emergency. For Aristotle, this was definitely not the case. That
thinker considered that to reach the goal of morality, we have
to practice every day just as an athlete or a musician does, and
this is called the practice of virtue. The task of ethics is precisely
to help human beings with this exercise.

Being virtuous requires assiduous practice. It is not enough
to have clear ideas; we have to exercise them over and over to
habituate our whole being to a certain way of responding to
reality. On the other hand, mere mechanical repetition is not

[10] P. Hadot, *Philosophy as a Way of Life: Spiritual Exercises from Aristotle
to Foucault*, Oxford 1995, 64.

enough to become virtuous. In this sense, Aristotle insists end-
lessly that each virtue is the golden mean between two vicious
extremes. The virtue of liberality, for example, is the golden
mean between stinginess and wastefulness. With this example,
the philosopher warns Nicomachus that moral life requires
measure. It is not a matter of blindly applying a norm or a rule
of behavior, nor of repeating a form of behavior mechanically
until it becomes a reflex, but of learning to weigh different
possibilities until we find the exact point of equilibrium. That
is why moral education begins with the formation of *phronēsis*,
in other words the practical intelligence that enables us to see,
judge and act adequately in the complex situations of life. We
learn to read situations, to situate ourselves in them and to
discover the possibilities they offer us; we elucidate the most
adequate action and undertake it with determination. The type
of intelligence that this whole process requires is different from
that used to solve mathematical problems or in speculative
philosophy, but it is also a manifestation—a quite valid one—of
human intelligence that must be taken into account. Ethics is
at the service of the development of this type of practical intelligence, required by the cultivation of virtue.

To understand correctly the Aristotelian concept of virtue,
it is important to realize as well the subtle relationship it has
with happiness. We have said that happiness does not consist
in achieving something outside the person; it is not a matter
of possessing riches, enjoying pleasures or being admired by
others. Happiness consists, rather, in acquiring a form of being,
a certain personality, and the virtues are presented as the road
to this end, but in a certain sense they also contain it: they are
not merely a means to an end in the way technical abilities are.
For example, knowing how to keep accounts is a technical
ability; liberality, in other words the ability to have a correct
relationship with money, is a virtue. The first helps me to acquire and administer an external good; the second is an internal good, forming part of who I am. Happiness consists in
possessing that combination of virtues that form the character

of a person of integrity; a happy person is not someone who possesses external goods—wealth, pleasure, prestige—but someone who has become just, magnanimous, courageous. A man or woman of this sort has accomplished what we can aspire to as human beings. For this reason, according to Aristotle, being happy is nothing other than being virtuous; the person who has achieved virtue has fulfilled in his or her being the possibilities of his or her nature. We call "happy" someone who has realized his or her potential as a human being.

Aristotle also recognizes something that everyone finds terribly evident: hardships of all sorts lie in wait for human beings. In fact, however much fate smiles on a person, no one can manage to be truly happy if she or he is not virtuous. Being virtuous, however, is not a sufficient condition, because sickness and misfortune can attack even the most excellent human being. In this sense, and beyond what fortune can offer, the only thing that is within the reach of human beings to achieve fulfillment is daily personal exercise, by which every individual strives to advance along the path of virtue.

Philia

The Aristotelian ideal of happiness is not a cozy nirvana of individual well-being. Aristotle is aware that without friends it is impossible to be happy. The human being is a *zōon politikon* (*Politics*, 1253a, 7), a social animal who by nature can only reach his or her end in society, in interaction with other members of the *polis* (*Politics*, 1169b, 17–21). The virtues can be understood in this framework and have to be cultivated in the real life of persons who are in relation with one another. Human beings cannot flourish or bear fruit in isolation, but rather by building with others a happy community, a city in which virtuous people are friends who work together for the common good.

Friendship-love (*philia*) is the third basic concept in Aristotelian ethics that complements the other two that we have examined. Of the ten books that make up the *Nicomachean Ethics*, two are devoted to it. According to the philosopher, friendship is "most necessary with a view to living. For without friends no one would choose to live, though he had all other goods" (*Nicomachean Ethics* VIII, 1 [1155a, 4–6]).

Just as with happiness, it is important to emphasize that what Aristotle calls *philia* does not coincide exactly with what we usually call "friendship." Today friendship is generally considered a private affair that cannot or should not be justified rationally; many people in our culture understand friendship, like happiness, to be solely a matter of feelings. For Aristotle, feelings are certainly an inescapable part of friendship, but friends do not choose one another arbitrarily. Aristotelian friendship has a political character; in other words, it takes its place within the interactions that are characteristic of the *polis*. True friendship can only flourish between persons who cultivate the virtues oriented towards the building up of society; in fact, only those who share the same end can be friends, those whose lives are committed to the *common good*, understood not as the goods that each individual enjoys, but as a common project whose promise of happiness is based precisely on the fact that it is shared by the community.

In the Context of the *Polis*

The vision of Aristotle concerning moral life is defined by the *polis*. Happiness, virtue and friendship can only exist in the context of the city-state, understood ideally as a society of friends who seek the common good, a community of men and women who possess the virtues that the construction of a shared happiness requires.

When Aristotle speaks of the *polis*, he is thinking of a specific structure of human coexistence—the Greek city-state. During the seventh century BCE, on the coasts of the Aegean Sea and in its many islands, a series of autonomous cities arose that were organized by different forms of government. They were small and participatory enough to be recognized by their members as communities whose destiny was in the hands of their citizens, and at the same time large and complex enough to allow a diversity of talents and abilities to flourish in them. This is the framework within which our philosopher understands happiness as the horizon of human potential, a potential that is realized when citizens collaborate, using their particular abilities, to build the *polis* together.

At this point we discover the basic difference between the thought of Aristotle and the ethical and political philosophies of the Enlightenment. In their intention to secularize ethics and politics, the Enlightenment philosophers eliminated from their horizon happiness understood as a social project shared in common.[11] The "pursuit of happiness" (mentioned in the Declaration of Independence of the United States) was turned into an individual affair. Each person is free to pursue happiness as it appears to him or her. The role of the State is to guarantee the freedoms and the rights of all, but not to dictate to them how to attain happiness. As long as they do not harm the rights of others, individuals can be happy as they wish to be and no one can ask them to justify this. In this way happiness remains inevitably privatized and excluded from the public forum and from rational ethical dialogue.

For MacIntyre, this lack of a common project is what lies at the root of the slide into nihilism of Western culture, especially noticeable in recent decades. This author, considering that there exists no political or cultural way out that could be directed by the State or accepted by society as a whole, draws the following conclusion:

> What matters at this stage is the construction of local forms of community within which civility and the intellectual and moral life can be sustained through the new dark ages which are already upon us. . . . This time however the barbarians are not waiting beyond the frontiers; they have already been governing us for quite some time. And it is our lack of consciousness of this that constitutes part of our predicament.

---

[11] Cf. R. Gascoigne, *The Public Forum and Christian Ethics*, 1–10.

> We are waiting not for a Godot, but for another—doubtless very different—St. Benedict.[12]

Is it necessary to be so apocalyptic? Is Western civilization in the final stages of modernity, heading so irremediably towards a new dark age? Certainly this possibility should not be discounted, but the future is not written in stone. The creation of "local forms of community" is certainly an inescapable step forward, but it is not the only thing we can do to keep our civilization from falling off a cliff.

I am convinced that pluralistic democracy is a historical step forward that we cannot disdain for the sake of a golden age that never existed. The way out of the current cultural and political crisis has to be sought—as the social doctrine of the Catholic Church has been proposing for more than a century—by inviting men and women of goodwill to find projects of social well-being that can be shared by large majorities; that is the framework within which the Christian message must be situated. Church communities cannot develop only by looking within, investing all their energies in creating a way of life safe from the supposed barbarism all around them; their role is to sow seeds of the Kingdom of God in the vast field of the world, and their proposals must go beyond the limits of the church, formulating realistic projects that serve as milestones on the road towards universal fraternity.

Much of the political philosophy of the modern world has aimed at supporting the legitimacy of the rules of the game that protect freedom and equality of opportunity for all, but it is becoming evident that an ethical dialogue that goes beyond an agreement on rules and procedures must be undertaken. In other words, we must also speak about the content of the common good, which cannot be understood only as material prosperity. The truth that "money cannot buy happiness" is also applicable in the social arena; the true happiness

---

[12] A. C. MacIntyre, *After Virtue*, 263.

spoken of by Aristotle and his Jewish, Muslim and Christian interpreters in the Middle Ages consists in sharing a social project, not in producing more and allowing individuals to consume their portions just as they please. The individualism of our culture has structural causes, and has to be dealt with politically as well.

We do not wish, and we cannot permit, the State to impose with its force of coercion a model of happiness obligatory for everyone, but this does not absolve the citizens from making the public forum a space of dialogue to expose, share and discuss our convictions about the "good life."

Experts of different tendencies today have offered their diagnoses of the crisis of solidarity in our societies. A philosopher deeply involved with the tradition of secularism like Jürgen Habermas has recently defended that "it is in the interest of the constitutional state to deal carefully with all the cultural sources [especially religion] that nourish its citizens' consciousness of norms and their solidarity."[13] In a truly pluralistic and caring society, it is not enough to tolerate one another; there must also be a dialogue about the purpose of personal and social life. Questions like "What meaning do I give to life?" or "What is my idea of a happy society?" must be brought back into the public forum, and it is there that we Christians, in all humility and without attempting to impose anything on anyone, have something to say.

The Concept of a "Practice"

As we have seen in the previous sections, virtue ethics presupposes a conceptual framework very different from that in which much of contemporary ethical thinking operates. For this reason, to understand it correctly it is not enough to juxtapose concepts like "happiness," "virtue," and "friendship"

---

[13] J. Habermas – J. Ratzinger, *Dialectics of Secularization – On Reason and Religion*, trans. Brian McNeil, Ignatius Press, San Francisco 2006, 46.

with others coined by the philosophies of modernity, such as "obligation," "values," or "utility." The concept of virtue, for example, can only be understood by returning to its original meaning and seeing it in the context of a teleological ethics, in other words as the attribute of persons who journey with others towards their human destiny or fulfillment, described by Aristotle as *eudaimonia*.

We have also seen that a basic difference between Aristotelian philosophy and the ethical schools of modernity lies in their understanding of society. One of the characteristics of modernity is suspicion of the State. Contemporary men and women do not live in a *polis* characterized by an ideal of happiness shared by all the citizens; in fact, in our individualistic culture, happiness is generally something that one enjoys in private. Fortunately, today it is possible to find social situations that awaken us to the experience of the good as a shared aim and enable us to situate ourselves within the coordinates that make virtue intelligible.

Aristotle uses the Greek term *praxis* to name this concept; MacIntyre calls it, in English, a practice. Unlike what happens with the categories of happiness, virtue and friendship, Aristotle does not treat it thematically, but as a reality that colors his discourse, something that belongs to the structure of the *polis* and for this reason is taken for granted. Here is MacIntyre's definition:

> By a "practice" I am going to mean any coherent and complex form of socially established cooperative human activity through which goods internal to that form of activity are realized in the course of trying to achieve those standards of excellence which are appropriate to, and partially definitive of, that form of activity, with the result that human powers to achieve excellence, and human conceptions of the ends and goods involved, are systematically extended.[14]

---

[14] A. C. MacIntyre, *After Virtue*, 187.

Examples of "practices" are architecture, medicine, agriculture, soccer, chess, painting, music, physics, and the automobile industry. Each one of these activities requires the participation of an organized community of persons, united for a common end. Each practice is characterized by the end that MacIntyre calls "an internal good": for medicine it is the health of persons; for physics, the mathematical description of nature; for soccer, to score more goals than the opponent.

What justifies the existence of a practice is its internal good: medicine is practiced to cure sick people, and one studies architecture in order to build beautiful and functional buildings. The participants in a practice normally are recompensed by external goods—money, prestige, or power. A physician receives fees and enjoys social prestige, and his instructions are obeyed by his subordinates and patients; nevertheless, what gives meaning to the practice are not these external goods, but the search for the internal good. The external good must always be subordinate to the internal good, under pain of perverting the practice. A doctor more interested in her salary or prestige than the health of her patients is a bad doctor, one who perverts the practice of medicine.[15]

Every practice involves a tradition and its apprenticeship requires the beginner to place him- or herself in contact with a community that incarnates and transmits it, since a practice is not only a mass of technical knowledge but also a school of indispensable virtues. A medical student can spend many hours alone in her room studying the manuals of the profession, but she cannot complete her studies without working in real clinics, in contact with experienced physicians; only from them can she learn compassion, prudence, scientific curiosity and patience, things that are just as important, or more so, than being up-to-date with technical knowledge. As Aristotle says, "by learning we do and by doing we learn." A practice presup-

---

[15] Cf. A. Cortina, *Ética civil y religión*, Madrid 1995, 22–29.

poses a living tradition by which "knowing what to do" is transmitted from teachers to disciples. And this is always much more than a series of rules that have to be obeyed or protocols that must be followed.

MacIntyre affirms: "We cannot be initiated into a practice without accepting the authority of the best standards realized so far."[16] Just as for a child who wants to be a successful football player, or a youth who tries to emulate an altruistic leader, in every practice those who act according to "the best standards" point the way forward. This does not mean, however, that models of excellence are fixed once and for all; the reverse is true. Those who accomplish a practice are "trying to achieve those standards of excellence which are appropriate to, and partially definitive of, that form of activity," with the result that the "human conceptions of the ends and goods involved are systematically extended."[17]

A practice is inconceivable without the internal good it pursues. This internal good is not something unchangeable, however; it is a moving target. The objectives of the team of physicists that found the Higgs boson in the LHC—the large hadron collider—were different from their colleagues who speculated about the structure of the atom a century earlier. The aims of physics have evolved within that discipline, because the answers to certain questions that were found opened new fields of inquiry. The same thing can be said of other practices whose evolution is less linear. This is the case with the arts: in introducing cubism, Picasso transgressed the canons of beauty of his time and his aesthetic proposal met with resistance in the artistic community, but when it was finally accepted, it caused the practice of painting to advance in a new direction. This dynamism of the ends is what distinguishes a living tradition from one that has turned into a museum piece.

---

[16] A. C. MacIntyre, *After Virtue*, 190.
[17] Ibid., 187.

A practice requires institutions to be sustained. MacIntyre is particularly critical with respect to them. In the first place, he warns that we must not confuse the two concepts: "Chess, physics and medicine are practices; chess clubs, laboratories, universities and hospitals are institutions."[18] Institutions are necessary to sustain practices, but at the same time they represent the greatest threat to them, because they are inevitably compromised with external goods: in fact, "they are involved in acquiring money and other material goods; they are structured in terms of power and status, and they distribute money, power and status as rewards."[19] No practice can survive for a long time without institutions. Nonetheless, as soon as institutions foster dynamics of power that distribute external goods above and beyond the internal goods that the practice pursues, they necessarily represent a danger.

The search for excellence determines the relationship of those who take part in the same practice: we exchange information, share concerns, encourage efforts, admire achievements; in this way bonds that form a community are created. It is not surprising that colleagues turn into friends. When things work, questions of money, prestige and power do not disappear, but they take second place; the community lives for the internal good and its members learn that external goods are at the service of something of greater importance.

Practices are the home of virtue. Since virtues are not cultivated in a vacuum, they must be learned in social contexts provided by practices. I do not acquire compassion by meditating upon it, but by participating in a disciplined way in a practice that puts me into contact with those who suffer and allows me to learn from those who have been practicing a concrete work of mercy long before me. By practicing compassion we become compassionate. By doing good we will become good.

[18] Ibid., 194.
[19] Ibid.

Jesus and Aristotle

Up till now we have been describing the main elements of Aristotelian ethics. Now we have to show how this philosophical framework can help us better to understand the Christian life. We will see that the concepts of happiness, friendship and virtue are very useful in formulating Christian ethics. At the same time, we Christians give those concepts a very different content from what Aristotle attributed to them, because our model of happiness is not a philosopher who was tutor to a prince,[20] but a Jewish carpenter who traveled through the towns of Galilee, "with no place to lay his head," a peculiar teacher who said to the crowds that followed him: "Happy the poor, those who weep, the hungry." There is no doubt that Aristotle would have felt it to be a folly (*moria*) to present as a model for human beings a rebel who died on a cross.[21]

Without a doubt, happiness is something very different for Aristotle and for Jesus of Nazareth, but for both the Greek philosopher and the Jewish prophet, it consists in fulfilling a destiny. The idea of happiness as a project spanning an entire lifetime is something we Christians find valid in the thought of Aristotle. Another element that we retain from his moral philosophy is that happiness pertains to the order of what a person is, not what he or she possesses.

Concerning the virtues, even if there are coincidences between what Aristotelianism and Christianity consider virtuous, it is evident that important discrepancies exist. In Aristotle's mind, the ideal of the perfect human being is a prudent and strong man capable of self-control and endowed

---

[20] Aristotle was the tutor of the son of Philip, king of Macedonia, the future Alexander the Great.

[21] The apostle Paul writes, "We preach a crucified Christ, a scandal for the Jews and folly (*moria*) for the Gentiles" (1 Cor 1:23). *Moria* can likewise be translated as "necessity, stupidity, insanity." The title in Greek of the famous work of Erasmus of Rotterdam, *In Praise of Folly*, is precisely *Morias Egkomion*.

with a sense of justice; among the traits of this ideal man, however, mercy or love for the poor are not found. Other basic Christian virtues like humility or faith are likewise absent from Aristotle's list. This does not keep the Aristotelian reflection on virtue from still having a great deal to contribute to Christian ethics.

First of all, the language of the virtues makes it possible to liberate ethical reflection from its restriction to specific situations. It fact, we do not exercise our moral ability only when we deal with difficult decisions; virtue has to be practiced every day, at every moment. In this sense, it is not only a moral decision whether or not to have an abortion, whether or not to take a bribe, which candidate to vote for in an election. We exercise virtue in deciding to get out of bed every morning. We form our character when we choose to do our work well or in the way we discuss the news of each day. It is not even indifferent to the formation of our character what films we choose to watch or how we decide to spend our free time. It is not a matter of exercising our willpower in "emergency situations" when moral duty becomes inexcusable, but of cultivating a lifestyle that educates our way of being day after day. This idea of an ethics that accompanies the subject in everything he or she does during the day corresponds to the Christian way of understanding morality, since the Holy Spirit is not present only in exceptional circumstances, but dwells within believers and assists them at every moment of their lives.

Another essential theme of Christian morality that virtue ethics helps us to understand better is the relationship between will and desire. In a law-centered ethics, the will plays the role of the guardian of desire; the will is at the service of the law, turning into a superego that oversees what we do and keeps us from realizing prohibited desires. Virtue ethics, on the contrary, teaches us how to reconcile will and desire: "We have to educate our desires, open our eyes to what we really want, free them from our petty pleasures. We need to desire more deeply and more clearly."[22] Christian faith believes that there is no deeper desire in the human heart than that of being united with God. For this reason, desire does not need to be repressed, but rather educated to orient it to its true end. Intelligence and will are not the jailors of desire, but its guides and assistants that level the road and help it to overcome obstacles. For virtue ethics, moral effort does not consist in a spasm of the will, forced to comply with the law, but in a patient exercise to fortify the muscles and allow the best of what lies hidden within us to emerge. In a virtuous person, will, intelligence and desire are allies that cooperate to bring the person to his or her true goal: true happiness, found in communion with others and with God.

The concept of friendship-love is another of the basic elements of Aristotelian ethics that is essential for understanding Christianity. If, for the philosopher, friendship is an indispensable ingredient in the life of citizens, for Christians it arises and is cultivated in the context of a community of brothers and sisters that we call the church. Just like the Aristotelian *polis*, the church finds its meaning in a common destiny, even if this is of a quite different nature from that which the philosopher understands for his city, since the good to which the church aspires is the realization of the Kingdom of God, already inaugurated by Jesus and set to reach its final consummation at the end of time in the new Jerusalem (Rev 21:1-5).[23]

Two intuitions of MacIntyre on the concept of practice are especially relevant for our reflection. The first is his idea of tradition. To be able to exercise a practice well, it is indispensable to be part of a tradition; in other words, we need to learn from those with experience the ends to which the practice is

[22] T. Radcliffe, *Afectividad y eucaristía*, at the XXXIV Days of Pastoral Youth Vocation, Madrid, October 8–10, 2004.

[23] Cf. S. Hauerwas, *In Good Company: The Church as Polis*, Notre Dame 1995. In his work *The City of God*, Augustine of Hippo became the reference point for understanding the church as a *polis*.

directed, as well as the virtues and abilities that lead to its execution. For MacIntyre, tradition is not a mere repetition of the past, but something living, and what keeps a tradition alive is the fact that the good which is pursued evolves in the course of history. The different practices of the church—we can think, for example, of the works of mercy—cannot remain alive if each generation does not cause them to progress. Giving food to the hungry today, for instance, cannot mean distributing soup at the doors of convents, as was the case in the past. Organizations dedicated to alleviating hunger—from food banks to groups that denounce the greed of unjust systems of economic exchange—need to refine and develop their methods with the objective of making this age-old practice relevant to a new day. As a result, tradition understood well is also innovation.

The second intuition of MacIntyre that illuminates an important aspect of the life of the church is his idea of institutions. Institutions are necessary, since no practice can survive for very long without them. Thus Christianity could not exist as an ecosystem of practices without an institution that regulates and supports them. But the institution is not the whole of the church; it is only one dimension of it. The institution is at the service of the practices in which all Christians are involved, practices that configure the people of God as a sacrament of salvation for the whole human family. The institution is at the service of this people and of the virtues and practices that define it. MacIntyre is aware of the indispensable quality of institutions, but also of the threat that they represent.

In this sense, the Catholic hierarchy and the persons who compose it suffer from the permanent temptation to undermine the practices that support the destiny of the people they serve. We should not forget that the only man that Jesus calls "Satan" was not the traitor Judas, nor the cynic Pilate, nor the cruel Herod, but Peter: "Get behind me, Satan! You are a stumbling-block for me, because you do not see things from God's perspective but from a human point of view" (Matt

16:23). He says this only a few verses after having said, "You are Peter, and on this rock I will build my church, and the powers of darkness will not prevail against it" (Matt 16:18). From the beginning until today, Christians dedicated to managing the institutional dimension of the church have experienced the temptation of being absorbed by the dynamisms of power, prestige and money by which the world functions.

The Christian community can be seen as a *polis* sustained by practices that are the school of those virtues that transform Christians into citizens of the Kingdom. In this sense, the church can be seen as an ecosystem of practices transmitted by tradition and supported by the institution, practices whose purpose is to configure a community of women and men in the image of Christ, a model of the human being who is fully realized and happy. Being Christian is inseparably connected to this activity:

> Christian identity is not primarily to be found in statements or debates or arguments, but in particular practices, commitments, and habits. Christianity is not principally something people think or feel or say—it is something people *do*. The narrative of the Gospels is the story of what Christ *did*, and what God did in Christ, and the scriptural narrative shapes and inspires disciples to go and do likewise.[24]

Long before the first dogma was formulated, even before the gospels were written, the first Christians lived their faith; they understood themselves to be active members of a community called to be the presence of the Risen Christ in a world marked by divisions and violence. Their convictions and their life were two sides of the same coin. We call moral theology the task of describing these practices and formulating these

---

[24] S. Hauerwas – S. Wells, "Why Christian Ethics Were Invented," in S. Hauerwas – S. Wells (eds.), *The Blackwell Companion to Christian Ethics*, Malden 2011, 37.

beliefs in such a way that they "help us to see how our convictions *are* in themselves a morality," for

> Christian convictions do not poetically soothe the anxieties of the contemporary self. Rather, they transform the self to true faith by creating a community that lives faithful to the one true God of the universe. When self and nature are thus put in right relation, we perceive the truth of our existence. But because truth is unattainable without a corresponding transformation of self, "ethics," as the investigation of that transformation, does not follow after a prior systematic presentation of the Christian faith, but is *at the beginning* of Christian theological reflection.[25]

Christian theology forms a unity. The division of labor and research in the centers of theological education today has distinguished different disciplines like dogmatic, moral and biblical theology. But each time we go deeper into one of them, we inevitably confront the totality of the task of what it means "to participate in the reality of God and the world in Jesus Christ today."[26]

Conclusion

In this third chapter we have examined the pillars that support virtue ethics. We have proposed the concepts of happiness, virtue and friendship as fundamental elements of a moral grammar that make it possible to articulate a comprehension of Christian life.

This conceptual framework not only does not do violence to the bible texts, but helps to express the fundamental biblical intuition that salvation is an integral transformation of human beings. Our bodies and minds have to be configured to the

---

[25] S. Hauerwas, *The Peaceable Kingdom: A Primer in Christian Ethics*, Notre Dame 1983, 16. Italics in the original.

[26] D. Bonhoeffer, *Ethics*, Minneapolis 2009, 55.

image of Christ by means of the action of grace bestowed by the Holy Spirit. But grace presupposes nature. The reflection of Aristotle helps us to understand the way in which we can collaborate with God as human beings in our own transformation.

We concluded, therefore, the first part of our book by presenting virtue ethics as a paradigm that can contribute to completing the personalist turn that moral theology has assumed as its task in the wake of the Second Vatican Council. As we set forth in the first chapter, casuistic morality, which dominated Catholic moral reflection since the Council of Trent, has been left behind.

These pages do not claim, however, to negate the incontestable value for ethics of discernment on laws and norms in concrete circumstances, since a morality that wants to influence real life cannot neglect the detailed study of particularly grave cases; there are things we cannot do without betraying what we claim to be. In this sense, virtue ethics does not contradict a morality of the law. In sum, while the morality of the law marks out the limits of the playing field, virtue ethics teaches us to play the game, because not only does it tell us what we have to avoid, but it helps us to think about what we can do and the way we should live in order to become fully Christian.

PART TWO

The Christian Life in the Light of Happiness, Virtue and Love

CHAPTER FOUR

Happiness

Happiness or Utility? That Is the Question

Aristotle affirmed that people cannot be happy without seeking an *inner* good. According to the philosopher, human fulfillment cannot be realized by possessing wealth or enjoying pleasures or fame. A truly human happiness can only be found within, in other words, in that which someone *is*, not in what they possess or enjoy. Being happy means acquiring, through education and practice, a certain form of being.

In Aristotle's ethics, the virtues denote the characteristics of the happy human being. The philosopher does not forget, however, that as human beings we are "social animals," and what forms us more than anything else are the relationships that we maintain with others. Only by interacting with others can we reach the full measure of our potential.

Aristotle imagined the ideal society as a *polis* in which its citizens took seriously the cultivation of virtue. In other words, they formed and trained themselves to be the best they could be, not only by developing their professional abilities and their technical capacities, but also by improving their moral character. For the philosopher, happiness is only possible when virtuous—just, sensible, courageous—men seek the *common good* together, a good which is good precisely because it is held in common. Being happy means becoming a worthy member of this city, built through the efforts of all.

The ideal society proposed by capitalism is fundamentally different from the ideal of Aristotle, because in it the concept of the common good is absent. According to the prevailing economic theory today, society functions because each person seeks his or her own interest. As Adam Smith said in a phrase that has become famous: "It is not from the benevolence of the butcher, the brewer, or the baker that we expect our dinner, but from their regard to their own interest. We address ourselves, not to their humanity but to their self-love, and never talk to them of our own necessities but of their advantages."[1] According to the author of *The Wealth of Nations*, the key to the development of peoples is allowing this free play by which each individual seeks his or her self-interest, because he considers that the combined effect of a multitude of persons, each trying to maximize his or her own benefits, will end up leading society as a whole to greater prosperity.[2]

It is true that, thanks to the market economy, we enjoy levels of material production unparalleled in human history. The free initiative of entrepreneurs is the main cause of the abundance that some benefit from today, but the prosperity advocated by the economists can never be equated with the *common good*

---

[1] A. Smith, *The Wealth of Nations, Books I–III, with an Introduction by Andrew Skinner*, Harmondsworth 1998, 119. The first edition was published in 1776. Although in *The Wealth of Nations*, Smith considers self-love as the exclusive motivation for human behavior, he begins his book, *The Theory of Moral Sentiments* (1759), by writing: "How selfish so ever man may be supposed, there are evidently some principles in his nature, which interest him in the fortune of others, and render their happiness necessary to him, though he derives nothing from it, except the pleasure of seeing it." This apparent contradiction is resolved by the current capitalist theory by omitting the assertion in *The Theory of Moral Sentiments* and considering self-interest as the only motivation that has economic consequences. The Nobel Prize-winning economist Amartya Sen tried to reconcile both of Smith's affirmations in *On Ethics and Economics*, Oxford/New York 1987, 12.

[2] D. Acemoglu – J. A. Robinson, *Why Nations Fail: The Origins of Power, Prosperity, and Poverty*, New York 2012; this work explores the relationship between free initiative and material prosperity.

defined by Aristotle, because it is not a project shared by the citizens, but rather the aggregate of the goods produced by them.

Economics owes much of its prestige to the fact that it is presented as a science similar to the natural sciences. What characterizes a natural science, however, is that the object of its study behaves in a predictable fashion, like the stars in the sky or the molecules in a chemical reactor. According to the prevailing theory in economics, what makes human behavior predictable is that people act in order to maximize *utility*.

"Utility" is the central concept of economics. It is defined as the quantitative value that measures the satisfaction produced by consuming a good or a service. It can also be defined as the quantity of means of exchange necessary to obtain these goods and services. Expressed more simply, utility is but another name for money and all that can be bought with it.

According to this way of looking at things, people act "rationally" when each individual adopts the most adequate strategy to obtain the most utility possible, given his or her circumstances. *Homo oeconomicus* is a predictable being, because he always acts "rationally," adopting the line of behavior that leads him to earn the most money possible and to spend it to obtain the greatest satisfaction possible.[3] Aristotle would not hesitate to call such people, who seek to attain external goods exclusively, irrational.

As a result, we are confronted with two alternative definitions of rationality. To illustrate them, let us imagine two brothers, two little boys fighting over the same toy. A mother who

---

[3] Behavioral economics attempts to introduce into the prevailing economic theory psychological factors that cause real behavior to differ from rationality, but it does not challenge—at least for now—the definition of rational behavior as the maximization of utility, but rather assumes it. A. Samson (ed.), *The Behavioral Economics Guide 2014*. Retrieved from behavioraleconomics.com. The Israeli psychologist Daniel Kahneman won the Nobel Prize for Economics in 2002 for his contributions to this new field, today in vogue, of behavioral economics.

would follow the theory that extols the maximization of utility would find the correct solution to the conflict between her sons by giving each boy a toy, so that each one can enjoy his own good without the loss of utility that sharing with his brother would cause. On the other hand, a mother attempting to educate them according to the Aristotelian vision of happiness would try to teach the boys to share, showing them that there is more joy in playing together than in each one having his own toy.

According to this latter way of coping with life, morality does not simply consist in obeying certain established norms to keep individuals who each seek their own interest from colliding, but in educating each person to discover a good beyond the self-centered enjoyment of goods and services. For Aristotle, the moral quality of a person is shown in his ability to learn to find greater satisfaction in realizing the common good rather than in individually enjoying goods and services.

At the beginning of this chapter on Christian happiness we turned to Aristotle, because his idea of happiness as a good internal to the person, one that is acquired in collaboration with others in pursuing the common good, is fundamental to understanding what we Christians consider happiness, especially at a time when for most of the culture happiness and utility are synonymous.

No one can deny that the economy plays an important role in society. It can help us to create more efficient institutions and to use scarce resources better. Nonetheless, an economic fundamentalism that sees the human being only as an individual producer/consumer keeps us from understanding the Good News of Christ, because the happiness of which Jesus speaks is not individualistic. In fact, faith is not a means of feeling better about myself or reaching a happiness in the beyond, a means which I would use privately. Gospel happiness is shared, or it is nothing.

Just like Aristotle, Christianity understands that happiness is a form of being that is acquired by committing ourselves together with others to something that transcends us. I can only be truly happy when I surrender myself to a project that is greater than the search for my self-interest. For the philosopher, this project was the building of a city in which justice and friendship reigned; for the Christian it is the Kingdom of God, which is also imagined as a city in the book of Revelation: "And I saw the holy city, the New Jerusalem, coming down out of heaven, from God, prepared like a bride adorned for her husband" (Rev 21:2).

Salvation is not conceived here as the ascent of individual souls going up to Paradise, each one enjoying its own private portion of happiness, but as the descent from heaven of a city in which happiness is a shared social reality. In this sense, Christian happiness has a *political* dimension similar to the Aristotelian ideal and is unlike spiritualistic outlooks principally concerned with calming the anxieties of the individual.

There is a difference, however, between Aristotelian and Christian ethics, since for the latter happiness is not conquered but is received as a gift, a gift from God.

A Concrete Proposal of Fraternity

To the question "What is Christianity?" many believers and non-believers would answer today by saying that it is one of the great religions, the one founded by Christ, understanding by religion something like a collection of beliefs about God and about what people can hope for after death, expressed by means of a host of rites and practices. This way of understanding Christianity is consistent with the way of understanding Christian revelation that prevailed in the Catholic Church from the time between the councils of Trent and Vatican II. According to this model, revelation consists above all in the transmission by God to the Church of a number of truths—the "deposit of faith"—that must be protected and kept free from all error.

As we explained in the second chapter, one of the great contributions of the Second Vatican Council was to achieve a deeper understanding of revelation. The dogmatic constitution

Dei Verbum understands revelation above all as the initiative of God who "revealed himself" in Christ to offer us the possibility of a personal encounter. No one is excluded; we are all invited to become part of this communion, which aspires to expand to include the entire earth.

Whereas for Aristotle happiness is found in the process of building the city, for Christianity God takes the initiative as the architect of this *polis* and places himself at its center, as the nucleus of a network that connects all the citizens with him and with one another: "I saw no temple in the city, for the Lord God almighty is its temple, as well as the Lamb. And the city needs no sun or moon to illuminate it, for the glory of God shines in it, and its lamp is the Lamb" (Rev 21:22-23).

Christ did not come to start a new religion, but to offer every human being the possibility of taking part in a communion with God that also brings human beings into a mutual relationship.[4] This is the meaning he gave to his life and this is the proposal to which we are committed if we call ourselves his followers. Christianity is not a system of ideas, and the church is not a club whose members find their identity in the orthodoxy of their creed. Naturally, the words we use to express our faith are important, but they are not in themselves faith. Faith is the active acceptance of the offer of Jesus to reconcile us with God, which makes us members of a community configured by a project he called "the Kingdom of God."

Brother John, a member of the ecumenical community of Taizé, defines the Christian faith beautifully as "the offer *in progress* of a universal communion in God."[5] By faith we do not only accept certain ideas; we welcome God in person who

---

[4] Brother Roger of Taizé (1915–2005) often repeated: "Christ did not come to earth to start a new religion, but to offer to every human being a communion in God."

[5] Brother John of Taizé, *Friends in Christ: Paths to a New Understanding of Church*, Maryknoll 2012, 26. In the original, the entire definition is in italics and not just the words "in progress."

reveals himself to us in Christ. By being in communion with God, we enter into a network of brothers and sisters that unites us with others. This proposal is universal, since no one is excluded, but at the same time it is concrete.

Christianity, before being a theory about God and human fraternity, is a concrete proposal. What we find at its core are not universal principles, but a particular human being, Jesus of Nazareth. In him we recognize the Son of God, who exists in a unique relationship with the Creator. The church understands itself as a network of communion, starting from Christ and under the impulsion of the Spirit, that spreads out from person to person in all the directions of space and time.

This concrete character makes the Christian faith problematic, because Christianity cannot take refuge in the limbo of ideas. It is not a philosophy that can remain unscathed by the way its followers live. The sins of the church are not only inconsistencies with respect to the proposed ideal, but objective rents in that network that interrupt its extension towards universal fraternity.

For the sake of truth and justice, it is necessary to affirm that Christians have done much good in the course of history. Many of the things that make life more beautiful and worthwhile today—cultural achievements, works of art, humanitarian institutions, etc.—would not exist if Christianity had not been around for the last two thousand years. But we must also recognize its errors and crimes, and the list is long. These acts against fraternity are a scandal for faith, as the Second Vatican Council recognized: "To the extent that [believers] . . . fail in their religious, moral, or social life, they must be said to conceal rather than to reveal the true nature of God" (*Gaudium et Spes* 19).

Nevertheless, these errors themselves are at the same time a cause for astonishment for Christians, because they reveal to what extent God has placed himself in the hands of a concrete community of fallible men and women. If the mystery of the incarnation fills us with admiration—God who emptied himself to assume the human condition—it is just as amazing to contemplate the fact that Christ turned the poor sinners who are Christians into his Body, and designated them as representatives of his project for humanity.

What should be the morality of a church that confesses itself to be the bearer of this proposal of universal fraternity? This is the question we wish to answer in this book. Christian ethics cannot, in the final analysis, be at the service of maintaining the established order, nor can its task consist in establishing laws of conduct that sustain this order. On the contrary, it exists to serve a plan oriented towards the future. It is the ethics of a group of women and men who have agreed to put their lives at the service of the dream of Jesus.

The faith of this group is not an intellectual assent, however, but a transformation that occurs in the contact with that God who has been revealed as Father, Son and Holy Spirit. The personal transformation that takes place in the members of this group is inseparable from their participation in a community that is defined by its mission: to reconcile the human family so that it becomes a reflection of that communion of love which is the Trinity.

Happiness is the name we give to the goal of this transformation. In this sense, happiness is a project that will only be fully realized in the Kingdom of God, but Jesus came into the world in order to tell us that it is possible to begin to experience the Kingdom here and now. Unlike the apocalyptical prophets, Christ did not predict an inbreaking of God to end history in a proximate future. His message is: "The Kingdom of God is at hand." The Kingdom of God is becoming a reality here and now in the transformation of people and their relationships. The resurrection of Jesus and the sending forth of the Spirit definitively inspired those who believed in him to engage with this vision. Being Christian is nothing other than learning to be happy, but the happiness shown to us by Jesus is just as surprising as the God who was revealed as Father, Son and Holy Spirit.

Father

In the prayer that begins his *Confessions*, Augustine of Hippo affirms: "You have made us for yourself, and our hearts will never rest until they rest in you."[6] The human heart is formed in such a way that anything less than God leaves a void, and this void causes a restlessness that motivates us not to stop until we can finally find rest in him.

Aristotle taught us that what gives meaning to the moral life is its orientation towards an end. In this respect, Christians have God as their end. Christian ethics is necessarily teleological, because the Christian life remains incomprehensible without this destination. In the modern age, the orientation of morality towards God became problematic. How can we be autonomous and free if we are subject to a Supreme Being that dictates to us what we should do? Immanuel Kant, the great philosopher of the Enlightenment, proposed that access to moral maturity involves embracing an autonomous ethics in which every person must discover what his duty is in accordance with his reason. A century later, the masters of suspicion would call into question the very existence of God. For Marx, Nietzsche and Freud, the idea of God is a source of alienation, an obstacle that human beings have to eliminate from their path if they truly want to journey towards their full emancipation.

Listening to these thinkers, Christians feel that the God about whom they speak has little to do with the One they have known through Jesus. Their suspiciousness only has meaning if we imagine God as an authoritarian father who mistrusts the freedom of his children. If God were a dictator or a harsh judge, it would be necessary to get rid of him to be able to live freely. In fact, for many people brought up in forms of Christianity that have presented this kind of image of God, atheism represented a path of liberation. And yet this is not the God we encounter in the pages of the gospels.

[6] Augustine of Hippo, *Confessions*, I, I, 1.

A fundamental task of Christians today is to share with our contemporaries the experience of that God who liberates, someone who, even in traditionally Christian societies, is a great unknown for most people. The Anglican theologian and bishop Tom Wright recounts an anecdote that illustrates very well what we are trying to say:

> For seven years I was College Chaplain at Worcester College, Oxford. Each year I used to see the first-year undergraduates individually for a few minutes, to welcome them to the college and make a first acquaintance. Most were happy to meet me; but many commented, often with slight embarrassment, "You won't be seeing much of me; you see, I don't believe in god."
>
> I developed a stock response: "Oh, that's interesting; which god is it you don't believe in?" This used to surprise them; they mostly regarded the word "God" as univocal, always meaning the same thing. So, they would stumble out a few phrases about the god they said they did not believe in: a being who lived up the in the sky, looking down disapprovingly at the world, occasionally "intervening" to do miracles, sending bad people to hell while allowing good people to share his heaven. Again, I had a stock response for this very common statement of "spy-in-the-sky" theology: "Well, I'm not surprised you don't believe in that god. I don't believe in that god either."[7]

The "God" that many non-believers reject has very little in common with the Father of Jesus Christ. I am sure that the future of the Christian faith will depend on how Christians manage to communicate the experience of having encountered the God who has come to find us in Jesus. Sharing this astonishment can stimulate a new conversation about the meaning of life on both a personal and a social level. I am also convinced that words are not enough, that only lives transformed by the

---

[7] N. T. Wright, "Jesus and the Identity of God," *Ex Auditu* 14 (1998) 42.

happiness experienced in the God of Jesus can give credibility to this *offer in process of a universal communion* that is faith. For this we need, in the first place, to allow Jesus to reveal to us the identity of the One he calls Abba, Father.

Paying attention to the way in which Christ presented his message is essential in order to be able to understand the character of the God who inspired his preaching. Jesus belonged to an oral culture and addressed himself primarily to peasants and other simple people in his surroundings. His favorite means of communication were the parables, little stories full of symbolism, forty of which were collected in the gospels. Still, the parables are more than a pedagogical strategy to be understood by an audience of people who did not know how to read or write.[8]

However educated and sophisticated we may be, to speak about God we need metaphors. Myths and symbols are necessary mediations to reach the depths of the human being and stammer some words concerning the One who is beyond everything. Paul Ricoeur coined the phrase "the symbol gives rise to thought."[9] Christ did not try to supplant one doctrinal system with another; instead "Jesus chose a form of discourse that appealed to human freedom." [10] These stories introduce the listener or the reader to an open reflection about God and the world. When we plunge into the world of the parables, our imagination intuits truths about God that cause us to break

---

[8] C. H. Dodd defined the parable in the following way: "At its simplest, the parable is a metaphor or simile drawn from nature or common life, arresting the hearer by its vividness or strangeness, and leaving the mind in sufficient doubt about its precise application to tease it into active thought." *The Parables of the Kingdom*, New York 1961, 5. John Donahue gives a commentary of this definition in *The Gospel in Parable*, Minneapolis 1988, 1–27. Concerning the characteristics of oral texts, cf. W. J. Ong, *Orality and Literacy: The Technologizing of the Word*, London 1982, 38–57.

[9] P. Ricoeur, *The Symbolism of Evil*, trans. Emerson Buchanan, New York 1967, 247–257.

[10] J. Donahue, *The Gospel in Parable*, 19.

with the divine image we are used to, and to recover the freedom to let ourselves be surprised by the Wholly Other. Only
in this freedom is a change of mentality (*metanoia*) possible
that opens us to faith in the God of the Kingdom.

In one of the parables, a king prepares the wedding of his
son and establishes a list of guests to be invited. Up to that
point, there is nothing special in the story. Something stranger—
but still within the limits of possibility—is that the guests make
excuses for not accepting the invitation. What is radically surprising comes afterwards—the king sends his servants out into
the streets to invite everyone they find: "the poor, the crippled,
the blind and the lame." "And those servants went out to the
roads to gather all they found, both wicked and good, and the
wedding hall was filled with guests" (Luke 14:21; Matt 22:10).
The extravagance of this king calls into question the image of
a god who privileges a few people or who rewards the good
and punishes the wicked. It allows us to understand that conversion does not mean adapting to a socially accepted moral
rectitude, but opening oneself to the question of how to please
this disconcerting king who invites *everyone* to his banquet.

Although preaching centered on the *Kingdom of God* is
original with Jesus,[11] many others before and after him used
the metaphor of a kingdom to refer to God. In the final analysis,
the primary attribute of God is presumably power and, for this
reason, it seems natural to speak of God by comparing him to
the authority figure par excellence in human society: the king.
In different cultures and religions, the gods are presented as
kings and the kings as gods. What was new about Jesus was
not that he spoke of God and his Kingdom, but the way he
imagined this King.

The other chief metaphor by which Jesus referred to God is
that of a Father. In this, too, he was not an innovator. Many

---

[11] The expression "the Kingdom of God" is not found in the Hebrew
Bible and only appears once in the deuterocanonical books (Wis 10:10).

religions call the deity the father of human beings;[12] what was original with Jesus was the way in which this image was portrayed. In his parables, Jesus tells of a father very different from the typical paternal figure in his culture. In this respect, perhaps no parable is more significant than that of the prodigal son (Luke 15:11-32).

In this well-known story, the younger of two brothers asks his father "for the part of the property that belongs to me" (v. 12). In that society—just as in ours—the sons did not share the father's property while he was still alive, but only at his death; but this father, against all expectations, gives his wealth to the son who asks for it. What happens then is quite unsurprising: the young man, who sees himself in possession of a fortune, misuses the heritage irresponsibly and is left with nothing. In his poverty he decides to return home; the story makes it clear that what motivates him is hunger, not nobler motives. On the way he prepares a speech for his return: "Father, I have sinned against heaven and against you. I am no longer worthy to be called your son; treat me as one of your workers" (vv. 18-19).

The surprise comes afterwards. The father, the true protagonist of the story, does something that is shocking in the socio-cultural context of Jesus and his hearers: he runs out of the house, falls on his son's neck and kisses him in public (v. 20). If running and showing such signs of affection outside of the home was improper behavior for an adult male, and shameful in a patriarch at that time, forgiving without asking for any

---

[12] The Old Testament is much more reticent in using the image of "Father" to refer to God. This reserve can be explained as a reaction against the use of the image of father god by the Canaanean peoples, the neighbors and enemies of Israel. The expression "father" applied to God evokes mythical representations that prophets and other biblical authors avoided. E. Jenni, "*ab*," in E. Jenni – C. Westermann, *Theological Lexicon of the Old Testament*, Peabody 1997, 10–13. For a deeper study of the idea of God as father in classical Judaism, see M. Pérez Fernández, "Experiencia y manifestación de Dios en la literatura y en la liturgia del judaísmo clásico," *Estudios Trinitarios* 36 (2002), 205–230.

explanations is a cause for astonishment in any age and culture.[13]

Kings and fathers were the authority figures in the ancient world. In the Greco-Roman society, as in most preindustrial societies, the two basic institutions were the household and the State. The first did not only fulfill the functions that correspond to the family today; it was also the basic cell of the productive network. Businesses and corporations are an invention of the seventeenth century, but before that all the work—agriculture, crafts and commerce—took place in the home. The word "economics" is a vestige of that practice that has remained in our language, because its root is the Greek word *oikos*, house.[14] The paterfamilias was, in this context, much more than the sentimental figure that he is today in the modern family, since he had the authority to organize work and the power to reward or punish the members of the household.

Calling God "King" and "Father" means recognizing his authority. In this Jesus was not particularly original, since any religion that takes itself seriously recognizes that the deity is a superior force with power over mortals; what was original about Jesus was the way he presented this father and king. He offers an image of God that subverts the human images of power: God is powerful, but does not exercise his authority like the powerful of the earth. Christ does not call God "Father" so that we may understand that God loves us as our father does; he does it to tell us that God loves us in a way that fathers

[13] Concerning the impropriety of kissing in public in Greco-Roman society, see the excellent article by W. Klassen, "Kiss," in D. N. Freedman (ed.), *The Anchor Bible Dictionary* IV, New York 1997, 89–92.

[14] "Economy" comes from the Greek words *oikos*, "house," and *nomos* "law." Economics is the science that studies the laws that make possible the correct functioning of the household, understood as a unity of production. In Antiquity, the household or the family was made up of the parents, the children and the slaves. In some cases, it could also include other family members and relations.

do not dare to do so in a patriarchal culture.[15] And he announces the coming of the Kingdom of God not to tell us that God will exercise power as a king would, but to show us that it is possible to exercise power as pure and disinterested service.

The modern world, whose great discovery is the value of autonomy, produces thinkers who advocated the elimination of the idea of God, because they felt that a relationship with a Supreme Being was incompatible with human freedom. In the presence of the Father and King of Jesus, however, we do not feel threatened; what fascinates us in God is his humility;[16] in fact, what causes us to turn to him is his disarming goodness. For this reason, any attempt to impose faith by coercion or fear denatures it irremediably. The road that leads us to the Good can only be taken in liberty.

Son

However original the images proposed by Jesus, what makes him unique is not that he spoke about God in a certain way. As we have repeatedly stated, Christian revelation is not basically the transmission of a doctrine, but the affirmation that, in Jesus, God himself has come to meet us to offer us his friendship. For this reason, believing means clasping the hand that has been held out.

Christ understood himself as the One sent definitively from God, who had to bring the history of the world to its fulfillment

---

[15] I think that this is the reason why Jesus preferred to use the metaphor of "father" rather than "mother" to refer to God. He wanted to subvert, in this way, the image of the authority figure par excellence in his culture. This same motive would explain, in my opinion, the fact that the father of the prodigal son seems to be depicted with the characteristics of a mother.

[16] "What fascinates in God is his humility. He never punishes, never domineers or wounds human dignity." Brother Roger of Taizé, *The Wonder of a Love: Journal 1974–1976*, London 1981, 104.

by inviting everyone to a great feast. He came to declare a "year of God's favor" (Luke 4:19) and to offer in the name of the Almighty a general amnesty that would make a definitive reconciliation possible. While he was walking along the roads of Galilee, he welcomed all who came to him, especially the sick and the excluded, but he was also the one who went to meet sinners, men and women who for some reason had distanced themselves from God.

It was a scandal for the right-minded people that Jesus forgave sins. "How can this fellow speak like that? He is blaspheming! Who can forgive sins but God alone?" (Mark 2:5-7). The parables of Jesus are a reply to the protests that his activity inspired. The evangelist Luke emphasizes this when he writes, "The Pharisees and the scribes were complaining, 'This man welcomes sinners and eats with them.' *So*[17] he told them this parable . . ." (Luke 15:2-3).

If Jesus welcomed sinners without requiring them first to do penance, that is because he understood that God is extravagantly generous with his forgiveness in this way: Christ's behavior is the incarnation of what God himself wants to do in this world. Jesus identifies himself so deeply with the Father that, in parables like that of the lost sheep, the two seem to merge into one and the same character: Who is the shepherd who leaves behind the ninety-nine sheep to go looking for the one who strayed, Jesus or the Father? The same thing could be said of the woman who, in the following parable, carefully sweeps her house until she finds the lost coin.

In this way the question of Jesus's identity arises. Who is this man who behaves in this way? Jesus himself asks his disciples this question at the center of the gospel: "Who do you say that I am?" (Mark 8:27; Matt 16:15; Luke 9:20). The first ecumenical councils, celebrated between the fourth and fifth centuries and which were decisive in the formation of Chris-

---

[17] The emphasis, obviously, is mine. Luke's gospel continues with the parables of the lost sheep, the lost coin and the prodigal son.

tian dogma, answered this question by using categories taken from Greek metaphysics: in Christ there are two essences or forms of being (*ousia*), human and divine, in one subsistent reality (*hypostasis*), a formula usually translated in the Romance languages as "one person and two natures."

Without these clarifications, very probably faith in Christ would not have been able to survive across the centuries in Western culture, built upon the foundations of Greek philosophy. Nevertheless, what we encounter in the New Testament is something more concrete, since the Semitic mentality, as opposed to the Greek, prefers to speak of actions more than essences. The gospels reveal the identity of Jesus through acts: he is the one who does what God alone has authority to do; he is the Son who incarnated the will of the Father.

The question of Jesus's identity was transformed at the end of the nineteenth century and the beginning of the twentieth into another typically modern question: Who did Jesus think he was? A basic characteristic of the modern world is its interest in the individual and in subjectivity. In this new cultural climate, the classical question about the nature of Christ, traditionally formulated in abstract and objective terms, is replaced by a question concerning the subjective perception Jesus had of himself.

Did Jesus's conception of himself evolve over the years? It is hard for us today to believe that Jesus had a full awareness of his identity and mission when he was still a fetus in his mother's womb, as some theologians affirmed in the past.[18] We take it for granted that the man Jesus grew, not just physically

---

[18] For instance, Saint Alphonsus de Liguori (1696–1787) wrote: "Consider the painful life that Jesus Christ led in the womb of his Mother, and the long-confined and dark imprisonment that he suffered there for nine months. Other infants are indeed in the same state; but they do not feel the miseries of it, because they do not know them. But Jesus knew them well, because from the first moment of his life he had the perfect use of reason." *The Incarnation, Birth and Infancy of Jesus Christ*, Brooklyn 1983, 227.

but also psychologically and spiritually, passing through the stages that every human being goes through, although the gospels do not describe such a process.[19]

With few exceptions—such as the scene of the prayer in Gethsemane—the gospels do not present the hesitations of Jesus either, something that would allow us to glimpse the crises without which no human being reaches maturity. We can only imagine them. The rabbis use the word *midrash* to describe a form of biblical interpretation in which the author fills in the silences of Scripture using his imagination. N. T. Wright does this when he replies to the question about the idea that Jesus had of himself:

> Jesus did not "know that he was God" in the same way that one knows one is male or female, hungry or thirsty, or that one ate an orange an hour ago. His "knowledge" was of a more risky, but perhaps more significant, sort: like knowing one is loved. . . . As part of his human vocation, grasped in faith, sustained in prayer, tested in confrontation, agonized over in further prayer and doubt, and implemented in action, he believed he had to do and be, for Israel and the world, that which according to scripture only YHWH himself could do and be.[20]

What was the awareness of Jesus? What would it feel like for someone to inhabit the body of a person in whom his disciples saw the very face of God? Our curiosity makes us impatient, but it would perhaps be better to recognize that the answer to these questions is found beyond what we can understand. We should be satisfied with what the New Testament assures us: Jesus is the Son in whom we can contemplate the face of the

---

[19] The brief notice in Luke 2:40 ("The child grew and became stronger; he was full of wisdom and God's favor was upon him") affirms the fact of the human maturing of Christ, but it is hard to see it as a description of this process.

[20] N. T. Wright, *Jesus and the Victory of God*, Minneapolis 1996, 653.

Father and the man in whom God's dream for humanity was perfectly realized.

At a certain moment of his public life, Jesus realized that a wall had been erected in front of him that impeded the progress of his mission: the system of worship established in the Temple of Jerusalem. Jesus was a Jew, and he believed what the Hebrew Bible revealed about God. It affirmed that in that Temple, and only in that Temple, God should be worshiped. Even so, the devout Israelite who was Jesus felt authorized to declare that that religious regime, which sustained the power of the priestly caste, was no longer in force.

He decided to go up to Jerusalem. Once there, "entering into the Temple, he began to throw out the buyers and sellers. He overturned the tables of the money-changers and the seats of the dove-sellers, and he did not let anyone pass through the Temple carrying anything. Then he began to teach them, saying, 'Is it not written: My house will be called a house of prayer for all nations? But you have made it a den of thieves'" (Mark 11:15-17).[21] Jesus could not have failed to know that by doing something like this he was risking his life. As might have been expected, the chief priests and the teachers of the Law came together at once to plot his death. On Friday of that same week, the body of Christ, naked and disfigured by marks of torture, hung dead on a cross.

Here the story requires a pause. We need the long silence of Holy Saturday to prepare us for the incredible surprise of Easter morning: Christ is risen!

That Jesus returned from death sounds unbelievable today, but it was no easier to accept two thousand years ago. The book of the Acts of the Apostles tells that, when the apostle Paul was preaching in the Areopagus of Athens, one of the emblematic sites of classical culture, the Athenians listened to him with interest until he happened to mention that Christ

---

[21] Cf. Matt 21:12–17; Luke 19:45–48; John 2:13–22.

rose from the dead. According to the text, "when they heard 'the resurrection of the dead,' some started to scoff and others said, 'You can tell us about this another time'" (Acts 17:32).

As long as the world lasts, the resurrection will never be something evident. It requires faith to believe in the testimony of those who affirmed that Jesus is alive, but it is this faith that makes people Christian. And as Paul affirmed in Corinth: "If Christ is not risen, then your faith is meaningless" (1 Cor 15:17).

Western art does not usually depict the resurrection and, when it does so, it paints Christ as a figure situated over the empty tomb, rising alone and victorious to heaven.[22] In the iconography of the Eastern European churches, however, the resurrection—*anastasis* in Greek—is represented by the image of Christ descending into Hades; there he takes Adam and Eve by the hand and saves them from death. This icon expresses the Christian conviction that Jesus conquered death, but also that he became the forerunner and guide of a multitude, "the first-fruits of those who had fallen asleep" (1 Cor 15:20). After our own death, we Christians hope to accompany the Risen Christ in his journey towards a new form of human existence that we cannot even imagine, a form of existence that God has prepared for those who love him (1 Cor 2:9).

Paul affirms that "if we place our hope in Christ for this life alone, we are more to be pitied than all people" (1 Cor 15:19). It is certain that the happiness to which Christians aspire is not limited to this life, but it is also necessary to affirm with equal vigor that it is not limited to the next life either: in the process of becoming more similar to Jesus, we can already begin to be what we will be forever.

Jesus recommended: "When you pray, forgive if you have something against anyone, so that your Father in heaven will forgive you your faults" (Mark 11:26; cf. Matt 6:12; Luke 11:4).

---

[22] For example, the works of Piero della Francesca, Matthias Grünewald and El Greco.

It is not possible to approach the God who is revealed in Jesus without letting ourselves be caught up in the dynamics of reconciliation that Christ came to let loose on earth.

He also said, "I am the vine; you are the branches. Whoever abides in me and I in them will bear much fruit, because without me you can do nothing" (John 15:5). Following Jesus means living in union with him. The happiness offered by the Christian faith is a form of being that we begin to acquire when, living in communion with Christ, we become involved in his project.

After the resurrection of Jesus, we are never alone in this process. We count upon the Holy Spirit, a mysterious presence, at times gentle as a breeze, at others noisy as a gale—of which the New Testament books speak frequently.

Spirit

When we enter the world of the first Christians by reading the New Testament letters and the Acts of the Apostles, we discover groups of human beings animated by an enormous creativity.[23] The protagonists attribute the energy that animates them to a new presence of God, the "Holy Spirit."

It is fruitless to try and determine where the action of the Holy Spirit ends and where human efforts begin, because God's power is not an adversary of human freedom, but rather its support.[24] In the early Christian communities, the Spirit was at work in men and women who carried a baggage of habits acquired throughout lives subject to the social dynamics

[23] W. A. Meeks, *The Origins of Christian Morality: The First Two Centuries*, New Haven 1993, 1–17; Cf. R. Stark, *The Rise of Christianity: A Sociologist Reconsiders History* or *How the Obscure, Marginal Jesus Movement Became the Dominant Religious Force in the Western World in a Few Centuries*, San Francisco 1997.

[24] As Luis González-Carvajal has written, "When God Works, Human Beings Sweat." *Esta es nuestra fe. Teología para universitarios*, Santander 2007, 126.

of the Roman Empire. The Gospel for them revealed itself as a call to attention that summoned them to rethink the patterns of behavior considered acceptable by the society in which they lived. An illuminating example of this is shown in the shortest of the Pauline epistles, the Letter to Philemon.[25]

An attentive reading of this short document—hardly a page in length—shows a fascinating human drama with three protagonists: Paul, Philemon and Onesimus.[26] Philemon was apparently a rich man who had embraced the faith as a result of Paul's preaching; Onesimus was his slave, who fled his master's house and came to the jail where Paul was being held.[27] There, through the apostle, Onesimus received the faith. Upon his return to the house of Philemon, this runaway slave brought a message for his master, which eventually became part of the New Testament. In this brief note, Paul asked Philemon to welcome Onesimus "as you would me." And he adds, "If he has wronged you in any way or if he owes you anything, reckon it to my account" (vv. 17-18).

The modern reader might perhaps find fault with this letter for not condemning slavery explicitly. Nowhere in his short message does Paul denounce the immorality of that institution; it would be a clear case of anachronism to hope for such a thing. Many centuries would have to pass for the idea of human rights to enter human history, and still more time for the first abolitionists to reach the conclusion, so evident to us, that slavery is incompatible with respect for those rights. The type of discourse employed by Paul is on another level. The

[25] N. T. Wright began his impressive study of Paul with a chapter on this letter. *Paul and the Faithfulness of God*, London 2013, 3–74.

[26] Paul probably wrote this letter in the year 53 or 54 in Ephesus, in the same prison in which he wrote the Letter to the Philippians. R. Penna, *Lettera ai Filippesi. Lettera a Filemone*, Roma 2002, 160. I heartily recommend reading this very short letter.

[27] Wright thinks that it was not by chance that Paul and Onesimus met in that jail, but that Onesimus went there to look for Paul so that he would intercede for him with his master. *Paul and the Faithfulness of God*, 7–10.

apostle's reasoning is not based on the inalienable rights of the individual but on the faith that assures him that Onesimus and Philemon are brothers.

In a subtle fashion, this letter allows us to contemplate the kinds of transformations that the Holy Spirit inspired in the households that became part of the great Christian family. There were scarcely any entrance requirements—owning slaves was not an impediment to receiving baptism for Philemon—but once in this network of relationships that was the Christian community, the faith began to reveal all its transforming power. Faith in the God of Jesus is not a static belief in certain truths but a dynamic activity of the Spirit that changes human relationships. Paul did not say to Philemon, "Onesimus has repented for having fled; I ask you to accept him again as your humble slave." This crisis did not happen so that everything would once again be as it had been.

Paul did not dictate to Philemon what he had to do, but he exhorted him: "Even though I have full authority in Christ to order you to do what is right, I would rather ask you out of love" (vv. 8-9). It is obvious that the minimum that he hoped for was that Onesimus would not be punished as the law prescribed (punishment for cases of this sort included the death penalty), but the apostle refrained from giving him a rule to follow. Philemon had to draw his own conclusions from the statement that the one whom society had made his slave was now in fact his brother.

Onesimus was brought to the house of his master carrying the letter. Now the decision was up to Philemon. Two possibilities were open to him: to tear up the letter, and with it his relationship to Paul and to the faith he received through Paul, or to welcome the message, and with it Onesimus.

I think that the fact that the letter was conserved in the New Testament shows that Philemon welcomed the second possibility and received his slave into his house. In addition, we have reasons to think that Philemon decided to set him free, something that Paul himself seems to suggest when he says at the end of the letter: "I have written to you confident of your obedience, knowing that you will do even more than what I tell you" (v. 21).

This example shows that Christianity was transforming society not by proclaiming great moral principles but through the practical discernment required by real relationships between people—husbands and wives, parents and children, masters and slaves—viewed in the transforming light of the Spirit.[28] This is what Christianity offered the world: not a theory, but a social space in which forms of behavior marked by the toxic manner in which the way rulers exercised power could be unlearned. And at the same time, the faith offered a space in which people could become accustomed to another kind of life bearing the stamp of God's power.

According to Aristotle, the search for happiness can only succeed in the context of a *polis* in which the citizens contribute to the common good, because only by being involved in the practices that the building of community requires can human beings acquire the form of being that is characterized by the virtues. For Christians, the church is that ecosystem of practices where we can learn the virtues of Christ. To the extent that it lives out God's plan, it offers that space to experiment with new possibilities that the Kingdom has opened up in the world.

The example of the Letter to Philemon is illuminating in attempting to see how the Holy Spirit acts to stimulate change in concrete situations. All the same, the place in the New Testament where the most explicit and ample reflection on the

---

[28] In Col 3:18–4:1; Eph 5:21–6:9; 1 Pet 2:11–3:12; 1 Tim 2:8-15; 5:1-2; 6:1-2; Titus 2:1-10 we find codes of household behavior that exegetes call *Haustafeln*, a term coined by Luther. These texts describe what relationships between husbands and wives, parents and children, masters and slaves should be. I think that these passages are a testimony to how the post-Pauline communities tried to reform the institution of the patriarchal family from within. On this topic cf. A. de Mingo Kaminouchi, "Pluralismo ético en la Biblia. El caso de la moral familiar," *Moralia* 29 (2006), 405–415.

gifts of the Spirit appear is the First Letter to the Corinthians, specifically chapters 12 to 14. At the beginning of this section, Paul reflects on what he calls "a diversity of gifts":

> There is a variety of gifts (*charisma*), but the same Spirit. There is a variety of services (*diakonia*), but the same Lord. There is a variety of activities, but it is the same God active in all of them. To each person the manifestation of the Spirit is given for the good of all. For to one a word of wisdom is given by the Spirit, to another a word of knowledge by the same Spirit. To another faith, in the same Spirit, to another a gift of healing in the one Spirit. To another the power to work miracles, to another prophecy, to another the discernment of spirits, to another different kinds of tongues, to another the ability to interpret tongues. All of these are the activity of one and the same Spirit, who distributes gifts to each person according to what the Spirit wishes. (1 Cor 12:4-11)[29]

Charisma (plural, *charismata*) in Greek means "gift, present." Today, however, we usually give this term a meaning different from the one it has in the New Testament. For the German sociologist Max Weber, charisma is

> a certain quality of an individual personality, by virtue of which he is set apart from ordinary men and treated as endowed with supernatural, superhuman, or at least specifically exceptional powers or qualities. These are such as are not accessible to the ordinary person, but are regarded as of divine origin or as exemplary, and on the basis of them the individual concerned is treated as a leader.[30]

This is the meaning we usually attribute to the word charisma today. We say that people like John Paul II or Barack Obama had or have charisma, which implies that most human

---

[29] See Rom 12:4-8 and Eph 4:16.
[30] M. Weber, *The Theory of Social and Economic Organization*, Glencoe 1947, 328.

beings are lacking in it. The apostle Paul, however, uses the term in precisely the opposite sense: every Christian has his or her own *charisma*, a gift of the Spirit. This *charisma* is manifested as a ministry or a service (*diakonia*) that the person accomplishes for the Christian community and the mission of the church in the world.

This is not the usual image we have of the church. In fact, the universality of spiritual gifts tends to remain in the background in most Christian communities with respect to the prominence of the clergy. All the members of the church, however, are unrepeatable and valuable. For this reason, to proclaim that Christians are children of God and members of God's people, without their participating actively in the life of the church through the exercise of the unique gifts that each one has received, means making a theoretical statement that, unless it becomes concrete in real life, can end up losing all credibility.[31]

Citizenship in this "experiment of the Kingdom" that is the church must not be a simple title, but the exercise of a personal responsibility. The first ethical urgency for Christians today may well be the recovery of spaces of community within which every believer can discover his or her own gifts and assume the corresponding responsibilities. When we are valued by our brothers and sisters for the *charisma* with which each person contributes to the common good, our dignity as children of God becomes a concrete experience.

On the other hand, a model of the church based on the passive reception of religious services administered by the clergy only reproduces the model of control and consumption characteristic of late-capitalist society. And if the first Christian communities were able to stand up to the domination of the Roman Empire, from the communities of today we have the right to hope for the same courage and creativity.

[31] J. H. Yoder, *Body Politics: Five Practices of the Christian Community before the Watching World*, Harrisonburg 2001, 47–60.

In this section of his letter, Paul continues to reflect on the gifts of the Spirit. In chapter 13 we find his well-known ode to the most excellent of the *charismata*—love.[32] The discourse culminates in chapter 14 in another theme—the gift of tongues.

Speaking in tongues constituted one of the most exotic practices of early Christianity. The Acts of the Apostles and this section of the First Letter to the Corinthians give us some idea of this phenomenon, but the references to it are contradictory. According to the book of Acts, after the coming of the Holy Spirit at Pentecost, each of the people from different nations gathered in Jerusalem were able to hear the apostles speak in his or her own mother tongue, a prodigy known as *xenoglosia*. This fact is presented as a miracle (Acts 2:5-13), as a one-time intervention of the Holy Spirit.[33] What Paul describes in his First Letter to the Corinthians is something different. The Christians of that community habitually "spoke in tongues" during their meetings. The apostle certainly attributes this phenomenon to the Holy Spirit; it is clear, however, that it is not something exceptional, but rather an activity that occurs each time they meet. What Paul describes in this letter is something scholars of religions call *glossolalia*, a practice that has been studied since the 1960s by cultural anthropologists.[34]

William Samarin, after analyzing the testimonies of Pentecostal Christians in Italy, Holland, Jamaica, Canada and the United States, described glossolalia as "verbal behaviour that

---

[32] Chapter 6 of this book deals explicitly with love.

[33] The gift of tongues reappears in two other passages of the Acts: 10:44-46 and 19:5-6. What is described in these passages is closer to *glossolalia*. *Xenoglosia* can be either a miracle or a way to interpret glossolalia; cf. L. T. Johnson, "Tongues, Gift of," in D. N. Freedman (ed.), *The Anchor Bible Dictionary* VI, New York 1997, 596–600.

[34] W. J. Samarin, *Tongues of Men and Angels: The Religious Language of Pentecostalism*, New York 1972. Felicitas Goodman took a further step in the study of glossolalia by extending the field of investigation to include non-Christian groups in Borneo, Indonesia and Japan. Cf. *Speaking in Tongues: A Cross-Cultural Study of Glossolalia*, Chicago 1972.

consists of using a certain number of consonants and vowels
. . . in a limited number of syllables that in turn are organized
into larger units that are taken apart and rearranged pseudo-
grammatically . . . with variations in pitch, volume, speed
and intensity."[35]

What this linguist is describing is a phenomenon that can
be observed in prayer meetings of charismatic groups. Some
people enter a kind of trance and emit sounds similar to spoken
words, but which do not correspond to any language. According to those who practice it, what happens is that the Spirit is
speaking through their mouths "with groans too deep for
words." The actors themselves generally do not know what
they are saying, but they claim that this experience elicits in
them feelings of joy and liberation.[36]

In his letters, Paul expresses the desire that all may have
this gift (1 Cor 14:5), and comments in his characteristic style:
"I thank God that I speak in tongues more than all of you"
(1 Cor 14:18), even though "I would rather speak five words
with my mind in the assembly, to instruct others, than thousands in tongues" (v. 19). In expressing himself in this way, the
apostle does not depreciate, still less prohibit, the practice of
this gift, but he dedicates an entire chapter of his First Letter
to the Corinthians to recommending that it be manifested in
an orderly way and in a form that contributes to the building
up of the community.

What could this strange message of Paul's epistles teach
Christian ethics today? Charismatic and Pentecostal groups

---

[35] W. J. Samarin, *Tongues of Men and Angels*, 120.

[36] Cf. F. Goodman, *Speaking in Tongues*, 24–57. According to a study
realized by single-photon emission computed tomography (SPECT),
during episodes of glossolalia reduced activity in the frontal lobe can be
observed, the part of the brain that deals with control of the will. This
may explain the feeling of "getting swept up" that the subjects report.
Cf. A. B. Newberg (ed.), "The Measurement of Regional Cerebral Blood
Flow during Glossolalia: A Preliminary SPECT Study," *Psychiatry Research*
148 (2006), 67–71.

insist that glossolalia should return to the liturgical life of the church as a sign of a renewed presence of the Spirit; most Christians, though, are unwilling to revive this practice. In the final analysis, during most of the almost twenty centuries that separate us from Paul, it has not formed part of the life of believers except in exceptional cases.[37]

"Speaking in tongues" is a spiritual technique, a method of prayer that enjoyed great esteem among the Christians of Corinth, because it enabled them to express a presence of the Holy Spirit that completely escaped their control. A religious experience where everything fits into a rational framework lacks, for that very reason, any attractiveness. The Spirit of God is at work in the depths of the human spirit, healing and transforming places that neither the reason nor the will of individuals can reach.

In the Catholic tradition, different schools of spirituality have cultivated non-discursive ways of praying that, like glossolalia, reach deep into our self beyond the limits of the conscious mind. The Rhineland mystics Eckhart and Hildegard, or the Spaniards Teresa of Ávila and John of the Cross, are masters who invite us to enter the "cloud of unknowing" to experience the Ineffable for ourselves. In a culture like ours, which leaves so little room for what escapes rationality, these forms of prayer are more necessary than ever.

Without depreciating the gift of tongues in the least, the apostle Paul insists that it must be subordinated to prophecy. "Whoever speaks in tongues does not speak to human beings but to God. For nobody can understand it; the Spirit says inscrutable things. The one who prophesies, however, speaks to human beings, building them up by encouraging and comforting them. The one who speaks in tongues builds himself up;

---

[37] Not even the New Testament—if we exclude the references in 1 Corinthians, the texts quoted from the Acts of the Apostles and a reference in the canonical conclusion of Mark (Mark 16:17)—contains any more traces of "speaking in tongues."

the one who prophesies builds up the community" (1 Cor 14:2-4).

The mystical experience must be articulated with the prophecy that backs up the moral task: "If I pray in tongues, my spirit (*pneuma*) is praying, but my mind (*nous*) is barren" (1 Cor 14:14). The spiritual experience transcends the human intellect (*nous*), but it has to be articulated with it to produce its conversion (*metanoia*), because the intelligible discourse of prophecy enables us to build together a community destined to be a figure of Christ and a parable of the Kingdom.

The Holy Spirit dwells mysteriously in the depths of our being. From a place that escapes our comprehension and control, the Spirit inspires a dynamism that transfigures us. This ineffable impulse, however, has to be translated into forms of rational communication and behavior that build up a community destined to be a sign of the Reign of God on this earth.

A Trinitarian Ethics

The happiness promised by the Christian faith is an offer of meaning, that is, of direction.[38] The Gospel confronts us with a decision: we can continue to revolve around our ego, satisfying trivial appetites, or we can provide an outlet for our most basic desire. Our faith teaches that it is by losing ourselves in the search for a greater good that we can reach happiness. The goal of this search is God, who invites us to take part in the communion which God is. To be at the service of his end, Christian ethics is not the account of a purely human effort, but moral theology; in fact, it speaks just as much of what God is doing for us as of what we must do to respond to the One who revealed himself as Father, Son and Holy Spirit.

By offering us his friendship, Christ Jesus invites us to occupy our place in the story of salvation that God is unfolding

---

[38] In Spanish, "*sentido*" means both "meaning" and "direction."

in history. Embarking upon this project, we find a purpose for our life, at the same time as we find ourselves liberated from the fear by which systems of power attempt to keep us under their control. The Holy Spirit configures us to Jesus's way of being, while inspiring us to create and maintain renewed human relationships. Taking part in the project that Jesus called "the Kingdom of God" and its unfolding in history constitutes our road to happiness, which will come to its culmination when Christ manifests himself at the end of time and we will then be "like him, because we will see him as he is" (1 John 3:2).

At the same time, the joy of God's Kingdom already shines out in the eyes of those who, by the grace of the Spirit, are converging towards the form of being of Jesus through the acquisition of his virtues.

CHAPTER FIVE

Virtue

The Beatitudes as Virtues

Happiness is not something external that can be possessed or enjoyed. Rather, it consists primarily in attaining the perfection of what a human being can be. The characteristics that describe this way of being and that delineate the personality of the happy human being are what are called "virtues." In this sense, following Aristotle, Thomas Aquinas defined virtue as *potentiae perfectio*, in other words the realization of a potentiality.[1]

Given that human beings are malleable by nature, they can improve themselves by education and training. From this perspective, the virtues indicate the road to such a transformation, and at the same time the direction towards which every human person must progress in order to reach fulfillment.

Just like the Greek philosopher, as followers of Jesus we believe that happiness belongs to the realm of being.

Nonetheless, and without denying this, we also think that the image of the happy human being has become incarnate in the person of Jesus. As a result, being happy means resembling him. Not, obviously, in what Christ has that is inimitable—a

---

[1] Thomas Aquinas, *Summa theologiae*, I-II, q. 55.

person with two natures, human and divine—or in his physical or psychological characteristics, but in his moral profile. The Christian virtues denote the moral personality traits of Jesus, which disciples must make their own. In giving a name to these traits, the list of virtues helps us to make more precise the reflection on happiness that we studied in the previous chapter.

In speaking of Christian virtues, there are three that immediately come to mind: faith, hope and charity, in other words the so-called *theological virtues*. This triad already appears in the oldest writings of the New Testament, in those where Paul speaks of believing, hoping and loving as three dynamic attitudes that converge to sustain the Christian life.[2] That being said, nowhere in the New Testament are faith, hope and charity referred to as "virtues."

We owe the concept of *theological virtues* to the genius of Thomas Aquinas. He discovered the structure of a virtue in each of the dynamic attitudes mentioned by Paul, in other words those habits of behavior that must be cultivated by exercise and that transform a person morally. In realizing, however, that there was something in these virtues not foreseen by Greek philosophy, Thomas felt obliged to qualify them as "theological." This adjective adds to the noun a characteristic absent in Aristotle that nonetheless remains essential for Christianity: the relationship with God. The virtues referred to are called theological "because they have God as object, foundation and end." In other words, "because they are in themselves a dynamic tendency towards union with God in

---

[2] In the letters written by Paul himself, the triad is mentioned in five different places: 1 Thess 1:3 and 5:8; 1 Cor 13:13; Gal 5:5-6 and Rom 5:1-5. In two letters probably written under the influence of Paul, they are quoted in Col 1:4-5 and Eph 4:2-5. They are also found in Heb 6:10-12 and 10:22-24; 1 Pet 1:3-8 and 1:21-22. In addition, in ancient Christian texts on the margins of the New Testament canon, they are mentioned in the Letter of Barnabas 1:4 and 9:8 and in the Letter of Polycarp to the Ephesians 3:2-3.

himself."[3] To these three virtues Saint Thomas added four others, which come from the classical philosophical tradition—prudence, fortitude, temperance and justice, generally known as the *cardinal virtues*. In adding to the number three, the symbol of the divine, the number four, the symbol of creation, the virtues of the *Summa theologiae* attain the number seven, the symbol of fullness. Aquinas thus integrates the four best "worldly" virtues of the pagan tradition and combines them with the three theological virtues in order to create the list of moral traits that should characterize the perfect Christian.

This catalogue of seven virtues is by no means, however, the only possible way of characterizing Christian happiness. In Saint Paul's letters, for instance, there are other lists of virtues. One example is the series of fruits of the Holy Spirit: "love, joy, peace, patience, kindness, goodness, faithfulness, modesty, self-control" (Gal 5:22). Another is found in the exhortation to the Christians of Philippi: "whatever is true, whatever is honorable, whatever is just, whatever is pure, whatever is pleasing, whatever is commendable, if there is any excellence and if there is anything worthy of praise, think about these things" (Phil 4:8). Thus Paul does not only invite Christians to adopt an attitude open to the culture in which they live, but he also calls them to incorporate into their own list of virtues those others found in the societies or the philosophical traditions that they encounter. This is precisely what Thomas Aquinas did by enriching the three theological virtues with the four cardinal ones.

In order to enter into the vast domain of the theological virtues, an ample and excellent bibliography is available.[4] But

[3] J. Alfaro, *Cristología y antropología*, Madrid 1973, 438.
[4] The bibliography on theological virtues is immense. A good place to start is the trilogy of encyclicals written by Pope Benedict XVI: *Deus Caritas est* (2005), on love, and *Spes Salvi* (2007), on hope. The encyclical *Lumen Fidei* (2013) was started by Pope Benedict XVI and finished and signed by Pope Francis. A theological presentation of the theological virtues can be found in J. Pieper, *Faith, Hope, Love*, San Francisco 1997.

for those who remain in our company, the following pages offer another route that also leads successfully to the heart of Christian happiness. Our proposal is in no way motivated by the desire to distinguish ourselves from others, but rather comes from having chosen a list of virtues to which the gospels accord primary importance: *the Beatitudes*.

There is widespread agreement that the Beatitudes are the basic reference point for Christian ethics.[5] And yet they are not always recognized as virtues. But if we define Christian virtues as the characteristics of a happy person in the image of Christ, it is obvious that the attitudes expressed in the Beatitudes are virtues. Jesus himself calls "happy" those who attempt to make their own these ways of being and of acting that he was the first to incarnate. The Beatitudes express as a true paradigm the moral traits that a Christian has to assimilate in order to be happy like Jesus.

What Is a Beatitude?

A beatitude, or more technically a *macarism*, is a name given to certain kinds of expressions that in Greek begin with the adjective *makarios* and that describe a kind of conduct or personal quality that deserves praise or congratulations.

A macarism was a way of speaking common to different peoples in the Mediterranean world of Antiquity; examples are found in Egyptian, Hebrew and Greek literature. In the Old Testament there exist about 45 macarisms, and in the New Testament, 37.[6] Most of the 27 macarisms in the gospels are

---

[5] The document of the Pontifical Bible Commission, *The Bible and Morality: Biblical Roots of Christian Conduct*, Vatican City 2008, quotes as an epigraph two fundamental Bible texts, one from the Old Testament and one from the New: the Decalogue (Exod 20:2-17) and the Beatitudes (Matt 5:3-12).

[6] The 37 macarisms of the New Testament are found in Matt 5:3-11; 11:6; 13:16; 16:17; 24:46; Luke 1:45; 6:20-22; 7:23; 10:23; 11:27-28; 12:37, 43; 14:15; 23:29; John 20:29; Rom 4:7-8; 14:22; Jas 1:12; Rev 1:3; 14:13; 16:15; 19:9; 20:6; 22:27. There are nine beatitudes repeated between Matthew

found on the lips of Christ, while a very few are spoken by other people, such as the simple woman who cried out when Jesus passed by, "Happy the womb that bore you and the breasts that nursed you!" (Luke 11:27). This is a good example, incidentally, to show that this kind of expression was current among ordinary people.

The first difficulty in understanding the significance of the macarisms is the word *makarios* itself. Traditionally it has been translated as "blessed"; this word is used in English today mainly by Christians, however. Since the word *makarios* did not have any religious overtones, translating it as "blessed" misrepresents the original tenor of the expression and gives the words of Jesus a pious note that they did not originally have.

For this reason, many modern translations of the Bible translate *makarios* as "happy." Personally I think that this is preferable, although with some reservations. *Makarios* does not mean "happy," if by happy we mean the state of well-being of someone who is enjoying life in a hedonistic manner. A macarism is not the recognition that a person is enjoying him- or herself, but rather a declaration of the person's excellence. Consequently, a macarism publicly honors a man, a woman or a group that, because of their state or their activity, has a value that merits recognition by society.

Over the last few decades, some bible scholars have begun to draw attention to the importance of honor as a way of understanding correctly certain New Testament texts.[7] These scholars

---

and Luke: Matt 5:3 // Luke 6:20b; Matt 5:4 // Luke 6:21b; Matt 5:6 // Luke 6:21a; Matt 5:11 // Luke 6:22; Matt 11:6 // Luke 7:23; Matt 13:16 // Luke 10:23; Matt 24:46 // Luke 12:43. Two of Paul's beatitudes are Old Testament quotations: Rom 4:7-8 quotes Ps 32:1-2. This makes a total of 28 different beatitudes, 17 on the lips of Jesus.

[7] A good example is J. H. Neyrey, *Honor and Shame in the Gospel of Matthew*, Louisville 1998. A background to these bible studies is the research of some cultural anthropologists, among which is prominent the fieldwork of the British scholar J. Pitt-Rivers in an Andalusian village, *The*

claim that in the coastal civilizations of the Mediterranean, and specifically in those where Christianity came to birth, honor constituted a value of primary importance. The anthropologist John Peristiany defines it by saying: "Honour is the value of a person in his own eyes, but also in the eyes of society. It is his estimation of his own worth, his *claim* to pride, but it is also the acknowledgement of that claim, his excellence recognized by society, his *right* to pride."[8]

Honor understood in this way is related to the modern concept of *self-esteem*, although with an important difference: in our individualistic culture, a person judges him- or herself worthy of self-esteem, whereas in the case of honor, the community decides who is deserving and who is not. Honor is consequently not a private affair; it is gained or lost before others, since it manifests the dignity of the person as this is recognized by society. In cultures where honor constitutes a dominant value, individuals are very concerned about how they appear to others: dressing appropriately, behaving correctly, doing everything possible to appear respectable. In these societies, gaining or losing honor—having a good or bad reputation—is a matter of life or death. This background helps us better to understand the Beatitudes: a macarism exalts the honor of a person or a group, and by proclaiming it publicly causes that honor to become even greater.

The Versions of Matthew and Luke

When we speak of the Beatitudes, we usually have in mind two lists of macarisms found in the gospels of Matthew and Luke.

People of the Sierra, Chicago 1961. Other voices have been raised against the abuse of this concept in exegesis, cf. F. G. Downing, "Honor among Exegetes," *Catholic Bible Quarterly* 61 (1999), 53–73.

[8] J. G. Peristiany, *Introduction*, in J. G. Peristiany (ed.), *Honour and Shame. The Values of Mediterranean Society*, Chicago 1966, 21.

Matthew lists eight beatitudes at the beginning of the Sermon on the Mount, the first and most important of the discourses of Jesus in that gospel. They are as follows:

> Happy (*makarioi*) the poor in spirit: theirs is the Kingdom of heaven.
>
> Happy those who mourn: they will be comforted.
>
> Happy the lowly: they will inherit the earth.
>
> Happy those who hunger and thirst for what is right: they will be satisfied.
>
> Happy the merciful: they will obtain mercy.
>
> Happy the pure in heart: they will see God.
>
> Happy the peacemakers: they will be called children of God.
>
> Happy those who are persecuted for the sake of what is right, for theirs is the Kingdom of heaven.
>
> Happy are you when people insult you and persecute you and say all manner of evil things [falsely] against you because of me. Be glad and overjoyed, because your reward is great in heaven; in the same way they persecuted the prophets before you. (Matt 5:3-12)

In Luke's gospel, Jesus pronounces four macarisms, collected in what is called the Sermon on the Plain:

> Happy (*makarioi*) you who are poor: yours is the Kingdom of God.
>
> Happy you who are hungry now: you will be satisfied.
>
> Happy you who are weeping now: you will laugh.
>
> Happy are you when people hate you, and exclude you and insult you and defame you on account of the Son of Man. Be glad on that day and leap for joy, for your reward is great in heaven, for this is how your ancestors treated the prophets. (Luke 6:20-23)

Both forms of the Beatitudes are different, but they have certain elements in common. Concretely, the first, second and fourth beatitudes of Matthew and the first three of Luke are quite similar (happy the poor, those who weep, the hungry). The last beatitude both in Matthew and Luke declares the persecuted to be happy. Most exegetes think that these similarities are due to the fact that Matthew and Luke copied a third "gospel" that has since been lost, usually called Document Q.[9] Each evangelist modified what he found in that text, adapting it to the particular circumstances of his communities and incorporating information from other sources, which would explain the differences.

In Luke, Jesus speaks to his disciples in the second-person plural; in Matthew, he uses the third-person plural. The formulation of the Beatitudes in Matthew is more elaborate than those in Luke: "poor in spirit" instead of just "poor"; "hungry for what is right" and not only "hungry." Matthew adds other beatitudes not found in Luke. On the other hand, Luke adds to his beatitudes harsh warnings addressed to the self-satisfied: the *woes*.

---

[9] An international group of experts spent years trying to establish the best possible reconstruction of Q (International Q Project). According to *The Critical Edition of Q* that they established, the Beatitudes would go like this: "Blessed are [you] who hunger; for [you] will eat [your] fill. Blessed are [you] who [mourn], for [you will be consoled]. Blessed are you when they insult and [persecute] and [say every kind of] evil [against] you because of the son of humanity. Be glad and [exult], for vast is your reward in heaven. For this is how they [persecuted] the prophets who 'were' before you." J. M. Robinson – P. Hoffmann – J. S. Kloppenborg (eds.), *The Critical Edition of Q*, Minneapolis 2000, 48–53 (the square brackets indicate a lesser degree of certainty). This reconstruction of Q supposes that Luke changed what he found in his source much less than Matthew; his formulation would thus be closer to the original words of Jesus. We cannot conclude from this that Matthew changed the Beatitudes of Jesus arbitrarily. In the first place, we cannot exclude the fact that Matthew may have had other sources of information—oral or written—different from Q, which came down from Jesus independently. In any case, Matthew's version of the Beatitudes forms part of a portrait of Jesus that the churches consider trustworthy and inspired, in other words—independently of the question of their literalness—they reflect a faithful portrait of Jesus and his teaching as it was experienced and recorded by the first believers.

> Woe to you who are rich: you have received your consolation.
>
> Woe to you who are full: you will be hungry.
>
> Woe to you who are laughing now: you will mourn and weep.
>
> Woe when everyone speaks well of you! That is how your ancestors treated the false prophets. (Luke 6:24-26)

In both Luke and Matthew, the Beatitudes are spoken to the disciples of Jesus. But in both versions they are part of public discourses—the Sermon on the Mount and the Sermon on the Plain—given outdoors. The disciples do not hear the Beatitudes in the private space of a house, but surrounded by a crowd of people. In this way they are presented as a "public theology" that everyone can hear. It is true that the disciples are the first ones called to put them into practice, but this tiny community has to see itself—in words we find later in the Sermon on the Mount—"as a city set on a hill" or "a lamp set on a lampstand" (Matt 5:14-15). The Beatitudes are a distinguishing mark of Christians, but not in the sense of a characteristic that separates them from others. Rather, they are a public message that they bear for all humanity. The Beatitudes witness to an alternative lifestyle that has been inaugurated by the inbreaking of God's Kingdom and that is available as a possibility and a challenge for everyone.

In this chapter dedicated to the study of the virtues, we will center our attention on the beatitudes of Matthew. The Lukan beatitudes declare happy the poor, the hungry, those who weep and the persecuted. These macarisms exalt the honor of people who find themselves in those circumstances and in this way they affirm "the fundamental dignity of the human being in the person of the most disadvantaged, whom God defends in a preferential manner."[10] In the Lukan beatitudes, Jesus declares happy those human beings who have the least, because

---

[10] Pontifical Biblical Commission, *The Bible and Morality*, n. 101a.

they are preferred by God, and he invites his disciples to honor their preference.

The conditions described by the Lukan beatitudes—poverty, mourning, hunger, or persecution—are not in theory assumed freely. One is poor, weeps, feels hungry or is persecuted without having chosen this. In this sense, the Lukan beatitudes cannot be considered ethical choices or virtues. Matthew, on the other hand, presents his macarisms as moral attitudes. Being "poor in spirit" or "hungry for justice" requires a determination of the will. They represent characteristics of a way of being that, in order to develop, require a commitment maintained over time. They are virtues that describe aspects of a lifestyle towards which we can aspire.

Happy the Poor in Spirit

In the Gospel according to Luke, the first beatitude states: *Makarioi hoi ptōchoi* ("Happy the poor"), and in Matthew: *Makarioi hoi ptōchoi tō pneumati* ("Happy the poor in spirit"). Both declare that the *ptōchoi* are happy, a term usually translated as "poor" but which refers more specifically to "the person wholly without possessions who must acquire the necessities of life through petition, hence those 'poor as beggars.'"[11] A poor peasant who earns his bread by his work and who, even as a result of hard labor, has what is necessary for food and clothing would not be described as a *ptōchos* (singular of *ptōchoi*). In fact, to designate the "honorable poverty" of those who live in a respectable austerity, the Greek language uses the term *penia*. The *ptōchos* is the poor person who has lost all means of providing for him- or herself—or who has never had any—and who depends totally upon the goodwill of others to survive.

---

[11] H. Marklein, *Ptōchos*, in H. Balz – G. Schneider (eds.), *Exegetical Dictionary of the New Testament*, Grand Rapids 1993, III, 193.

In this sense, to declare *makarioi* the *ptōchoi* is an obvious paradox. In fact, every macarism exalts the honor or the value attributed to an individual by the society to which he or she belongs. The term *ptōchos*, however, is applied to someone who has no value because he or she represents a burden to society, having no means to contribute to the well-being of all, and is thus a source of shame for the group. And it is precisely those people whom Jesus calls happy.

In Luke's gospel, Jesus declares the poor happy, and nothing more. The poverty referred to includes both the voluntary sort, that in which the disciples of Jesus find themselves because they left everything to follow him, and especially that of so many others placed by life in such a situation without having chosen it. Matthew's gospel adds to this beatitude an enigmatic phrase: *tō pneumati*. *Pneumati* is the dative of the noun *pneuma*, which means "spirit," and *tō* is the definite article that accompanies it. In what way does *tō pneumati* qualify *ptōchoi*? It is clear that Matthew wants to specify that Christian poverty is not exactly to be identified with material poverty but is rather a "spiritual" poverty. But in what sense?

Different interpretations of this have been proposed down through the centuries. Some have considered *ptōchoi tō pneumati* as people lacking in intelligence, in other words the simpleminded. Others have maintained that "the poor in spirit" should be opposed to "material poverty"; in this way, "the poor in spirit" would be those who live with no attachment to their own wealth, however great it may in fact be.

Both opinions are inadmissible. It is clear that there are people with intellectual handicaps who have a special capacity to love and be loved—and in this sense they are *makarioi*—but Jesus cannot be referring to a specific group of people with particular mental characteristics. As for the attempt to understand the beatitude concerning poverty in spirit as a mere inner attitude that does not interfere in practice with possessing wealth, this has all the earmarks of a subterfuge that would exempt someone from the essential commitments of the

Gospel.[12] We need only to remember the many sayings of Jesus concerning the dangers of riches to disqualify the juggling act that consists in making the unruffled possession of great wealth compatible with the beatitude of poverty.

Another option favored by some exegetes is to understand *tō pneumati* as an instrumental dative. In this sense, "poor in spirit" would be those who have become poor by using their spirit, understood here as the human faculty of making decisions. Expressed more simply, "the poor in spirit" would be those who have chosen poverty through an exercise of their will (= spirit). Following this interpretation, certain versions of the Bible translate the first beatitude of Matthew as "Happy those who choose to be poor."[13] This reading has had its partisans in the history of exegesis, particularly in the monastic tradition, but some acknowledged specialists reject as forced the interpretation of *tō pneumati* as an instrumental dative expressing free choice.[14]

Most bible scholars are inclined to interpret "the poor in spirit" as "those who live in a precarious situation and, above all, acknowledge that they themselves have nothing, are wholly dependent on God."[15] This reading, already found in the church fathers, enjoyed greater credibility through the discovery in 1947 of the Qumran manuscripts. In one of the texts we find the Hebrew expression *anawe ruah*, which is

---

[12] Luis González-Carvajal comments ironically: "This interpretation is very gratifying to well-to-do Christians because, with the excuse that they are not attached to their wealth, it enables them to keep on living comfortably and enjoying what they have. In this way they convert the beatitude of the poor in spirit into, in the words of Guardini, 'the pious embellishment of a life of plenty.'" *Las bienaventuranzas, una contracultura que humaniza*, Santander 2014, 57.

[13] This is true of the *Nueva Biblia Española*, one of the versions that had the greatest influence in the Spanish-speaking world in the last decades of the past century.

[14] U. Luz, *Matthew 1–7: A Commentary*, Edinburgh 1989, 232–234; H. D. Betz – Y. A. Collins, *The Sermon on the Mount: A Commentary on the Sermon on the Mount*, Minneapolis 1995, 112.

[15] Pontifical Bible Commission, *The Bible and Morality*, n. 47.

equivalent to *ptōchoi tō pneumati*.[16] According to that text, "poverty in spirit" defines the attitude of the members of the Jewish group that authored those manuscripts, who were waiting in the desert for God to intervene in their favor.

Someone "poor in spirit" is a person who stands before God as a beggar. This is the attitude of those who pray saying, "I have nothing and I can do nothing, Lord, but you can do everything; help me!" It is a matter, therefore, of confessing before God that we cannot reach happiness by ourselves, and humbly asking God to grant it to us as a gift. According to Jesus, this attitude offers us access to God's Kingdom here and now: the poor in spirit can consider themselves happy, because the Kingdom is theirs, in the present moment.

Jesus's preaching centered on the Kingdom or Reign of God. Unlike the apocalyptic prophets, who announced a divine intervention in an imminent future, Jesus declared that the Kingdom was an already present reality that was transforming people and their relationships, thus changing the world. Although only at the end of time would the Kingdom be evident to all, it was *already* breaking into the world in seminal fashion, so that people could begin to take part in it. Poverty in spirit, understood as a complete and radical openness to the God who comes to take control of reality, exemplifies that change of mentality—*metanoia*—that opens the gates of the Kingdom.

If we attempt to translate into our contemporary sensibility this attitude of neediness before God that Matthew calls "poverty in spirit," it is instructive to examine a situation that often is a cause of suffering today—*addictions*. The word "poor" acquires a particular intensity when it is applied to men and women who live as slaves of drugs or alcohol, or who suffer

---

[16] H. D. Betz – Y. A. Collins, *The Sermon on the Mount*, 116. Against this identification, U. Luz, *Matthew 1–7: A Commentary*, 233. The text in question is 1QM, 14, 7. *Anawe* is the construct form of *anawim*; *ruah* means "spirit."

from similar forms of self-destructive behavior. It is not infrequent that such people end up in the most absolute indigence, even though the greatest problem of addicts—as those who enter into a process of rehabilitation recognize—is the existential self-deception in which they live. The extreme stimulation provided by drugs, gambling or compulsive sex allows them briefly to escape the anguish caused by the problems of life; those fleeting moments, however, end up by surrendering to these substances or forms of behavior the key to their own freedom. Addicts deceive themselves by saying that they can stop whenever they wish, while a chain of lies takes them further and further away from reality.

A good starting-point to escape addiction lies in recognizing that one is powerless to control it.[17] The addict who wants to be rehabilitated must convince himself that his problem is not something outside himself, but that it belongs to his very being—the lack of freedom to take charge of himself in the face of the onslaught of the addiction. The solution is found precisely in this recognition and in the decision to display his own wound before the merciful eyes of others (and also, above all, of the Other), like a beggar asking for help. This acceptance of neediness enables the addict to break the cycle of falsehood and confront the truth, enabling him to realize that he does not possess the key to his own happiness, and the substances or behaviors to which he is addicted only serve to hide this inability. However, it is before God that the addict can best

---

[17] In this sense, the first of the twelve steps that Alcoholics Anonymous proposes as a road to rehabilitation lies in admitting one's own powerlessness with respect to alcohol and confessing that "our lives have become unmanageable." The second step is the theoretical affirmation that there exists a "higher Power" that cares for us and can help us. The third step is the hinge of the program: "We make a decision to turn our will and our lives over to the care of God." The following nine steps work out this third step. Other addictions have also been treated successfully using this method.

recognize that he is unable to attain happiness by himself. This realization is then transformed into a true starting-point and the real possibility of beginning the road back to reality.

We have taken addiction as an example of those situations in which poverty in spirit is revealed and proclaimed as blessed in the contemporary world for many men and women who are seeking their redemption. Addictions, however, are not the only case of self-deception that cuts people off from truth and ends in unhappiness. The accumulation of wealth is one of the most common forms through which many human beings try to make themselves safe from the possible reversals of life and the insidious feeling of not having enough for what they fantasize as a full existence. Money, however, never fulfills its promise to keep us safe, because we can never have enough of it. Often, the spiral of aspiring to possess more and more follows the same pattern as the dynamic of addictions: it is necessary constantly to increase the amount in order to calm anxiety. But unlike drugs, money has no limit that causes death by overdose.

All of us are to some extent addicts who try by all possible means not to accept our condition as *ptōchoi*. We cover the nakedness of our indigence, if not with money, then with other things that make us feel safe: fame, recognition, good jobs or anything else that testifies to ourselves and others that we are valuable and deserve to be loved. The good news is that we do not need any of this, because God loves all persons as they are, in their bare humanity. The only thing we accomplish by masking our radical neediness is to distance ourselves from God and from the truth about ourselves.

We begin to be "poor in spirit" when we open ourselves to the fragility of what we are and so make it possible for God to reveal his overflowing generosity and salvation.

At the same time, welcoming this God revealed in Jesus is inseparable from an effective solidarity with human beings who suffer, since the poverty in spirit that leads to a communion with God impels us also to open the door of our hearts to the multitudes who suffer due to a lack of the most basic means of subsistence. The Gospel promises the happiness of a life without fear to those who choose to share: "Don't be afraid, little flock; your Father has seen fit to give you the Kingdom. Sell your possessions and give alms. Make for yourselves purses that do not wear out, an inexhaustible treasure in heaven, where thieves do not break in nor moths consume" (Luke 12:32–33).

Aristotle would not have called poverty in spirit a virtue, even after a night spent in philosophical dialogues washed down with an abundant supply of wine. For him, virtue had to do with effort and intelligence, with human excellence acquired through talent and hard work. On the contrary, the first beatitude declares that the road to happiness opens up only for those who are ready to recognize that, in the final analysis, no human effort can make them happy and that to beg for God's generosity is the only possible way. In this sense, Christians are right to call poverty in spirit a virtue, because it is the basic choice that configures us inwardly as believers, a choice that cannot be made only once, but must be faced again and again until it becomes part of who we are.

Happy Those Who Weep

Matthew's beatitudes are not a collection of disparate virtues; they have a principle that unifies them. According to Ambrose of Milan, the macarism of poverty is, beyond being the first in order, the wellspring from which the rest of the virtues spring up.[18] According to this, the following three beatitudes are echoes of the first, each one focusing on one of its aspects.

---

[18] "Ordine enim prima est et parens quaedam generatioque *virtutum*," Ambrose of Milan, *In Lucam* 5.51, quoted in H. D. Betz – A. Y. Collins, *The Sermon on the Mount*, 111; the italics are mine.

The order of Matthew's second and third beatitudes is a problem debated by experts, since in some manuscripts—a minority—the beatitude of non-violence precedes that of weeping. Here we adopt the order that the Nestlé-Aland critical edition—the one followed by most New Testament scholars—considers most probable. According to this edition, Matthew's second beatitude says this: *Makarioi hoi penthountes hoti autoi paraklēthēsontai*, which we translate as: "Happy those who mourn (*penthountes*): they will be comforted." This macarism has a parallel in Luke: "Happy you who are weeping (*klaiontes*) now: you will laugh." In this version of the beatitude, the Greek verb that we find in the original is *klaiō*, which means "to weep" or "to lament." Luke sets opposite this the future verb "you will laugh," and by so doing juxtaposes the present suffering of the poor to the coming gladness they will enjoy. The Third Gospel thus announces the "eschatological inversion" that will occur at the end of time, when rich and poor change places.

Matthew chose different verbs from those selected by Luke in his version of this beatitude. Instead of *klaiō*, Matthew prefers *pentheō*, a synonym that means "to weep, be sad, be in mourning." In Luke, Jesus speaks to those who live the Beatitudes: "you will laugh" (*gelasete*), whereas in Matthew it is stated that "they will be comforted" (*paraklēthēsontai*). It does not seem that Matthew used these two terms casually; rather, we believe that the verbs *pentheō* and *parakaleō* have been chosen by this evangelist, who stands out as one of the inspired authors most familiar with the Old Testament, to allow one of the Old Testament texts most important for the early Christians to resonate in this beatitude, Isaiah 61:1-3:

> The Spirit of the Lord is upon me,
> because he has anointed me
> to bring good news to the poor.
> He has sent me to bind up the broken-hearted,
> to proclaim release to captives

and freedom to prisoners,
to proclaim a year of the Lord's favor
and a day of vengeance for our God,
to comfort all those who mourn,
to provide for those who mourn in Zion,
giving them a turban instead of ashes,
the oil of gladness instead of mourning
and a mantle of praise instead of a listless spirit.

The first readers of the New Testament knew the Old primarily through a Greek translation called the *Septuagint*. In that version, the phrase of Isaiah that we translated above as "to comfort all those who mourn" is given in this way: *parakalesai pantas tous penthountas*. The verbs *pentheō* (to mourn) and *parakaleō* (to comfort) of the second beatitude echo those used in this phrase of Isaiah.[19]

This prophecy is also quoted in the Gospel according to Saint Luke at the beginning of Jesus's ministry. Christ reads part of this text in the synagogue of Nazareth and adds, "Today this passage of Scripture you have just heard has been fulfilled" (Luke 4:18-21). In different ways, both Matthew and Luke present Jesus as the one who brings this vision to fulfillment: he is the Christ—God's Anointed—sent to comfort those who mourn. In this sense, the second beatitude of Matthew, like its parallel in Luke, is a declaration of God's preference for those who suffer. To be Christian means believing in the God who sent Jesus to proclaim good news to the poor. The ethical consequence is clear: Christians have to imitate this predilection of God for those who are in bad shape. In the context of Matthew's beatitudes, which present a list of virtues for the Christian community, we can discover an additional nuance: in publicly proclaiming *makarios* to the sad, this gospel invites us to become men and women able to share their tears.

[19] H. D. Betz – A. Y. Collins, *The Sermon on the Mount*, 121.

By this we do not mean to say, of course, that sadness is a Christian ideal. On the contrary, joy is one of the signs that distinguish those who have believed in the Good News of Jesus. At the end of the Beatitudes, Jesus enjoins his disciples to leap for joy. The apostle Paul writes in the same vein: "Always be joyful in the Lord; I will say it again, be joyful!" (Phil 4:4). Sadness is not something desirable, but by declaring that lamenting is something honorable, Jesus invites us not to hide our sorrow and suffering.

The verb "to weep" (*pentheō*), used by Matthew, refers especially to the experience of grief, the sorrow that accompanies the loss of someone dear to us. In our Western societies, mourning has become more and more a private affair. Funeral homes designed to resemble airports welcome the departed to expedite the most unavoidable rites and help friends and family to "turn the page" as quickly as possible. But without the necessary process of healing, the wound left by the loss can become a chronic ailment.

In order to assist many people who have difficulties with grief, groups are springing up to accompany them, especially in those cases where the loss of a loved one took place in a particularly traumatic manner (death by accident or suicide, the loss of a child). Those involved in this work speak of mourning as a process that, if conducted in the right way, can be fundamentally humanizing.[20]

All who love are fated to weep, because sooner or later they will lose those they love (or those they love will lose them!). Grief is the *a posteriori* recognition of this *having loved*, and the present awareness of the loss, which instructs us in the truth of what we are as human beings who are fragile and yet able

[20] "Losing a loved one can be the cause of the greatest unhappiness, a major trauma of life, with its destructive power. And it can also be an opportunity. An opportunity because dying and death require us to learn truth and truths, and can contribute to making us more human." J. C. Bermejo, *Estoy en duelo*, Madrid 2013, 12.

to love. Happy those who recognize this condition and cultivate the ability to express the sorrow that is born of a lost love,
because God himself will comfort them![21] The book of Revelation imagines the Lord wiping away tears with tenderness:

> And I heard a loud voice from the throne saying, "Here is
> the dwelling of God with human beings, and he will dwell
> with them, and they will be his people and God himself will
> be with them, and he will wipe every tear from their eyes.
> And there will be no more death, no longer any weeping
> and crying and sorrow, for the former things have passed
> away." (Rev 21:3-4)

That is the definitive comfort we are longing for. And yet this
hope, far from distracting us from the commitments of the
present, enables us to understand how essential it is to create
those bonds of love that will be the raw material for the definitive transformation. In this way we discover that, although
all the virtues are social, the virtue of knowing how to weep
is so in a particular fashion. The community formed by this
beatitude is that in which I do not always need to appear strong
and assured, because it is made up of relationships of trust in
which I can dare to reveal my difficulties.

The weeping to which the second beatitude refers also includes tears for other losses, for other situations in which
people have left us or we have lost something valuable that
made life more beautiful. If the first beatitude calls "happy"
those who stand before God as poor people, the second invites
us to express this poverty by weeping, or through other acts
by which we recognize that we are not in good shape and in
need of comfort. This comfort, and not the weeping, is the
cause of the beatitude, a comfort that comes from God, but

---

[21] The verbal form "will be comforted" (*paraklēthēsontai*) used in the
beatitude is a "divine passive," a way of expressing that God is the agent,
in this case of the comfort.

also from those who are part of that special human community destined to be a sign of God's Kingdom on earth. We can only say "happy those who weep" without cynicism when we offer our shoulder to those who are in mourning so that they can shed their tears on it.

Happy the Non-Violent

The third beatitude in Matthew's list says, in the original Greek of the New Testament: *Makarioi hoi praeis, hoti autoi klēronomēsousin tēn gēn*, "happy the *praeis*: they will inherit the earth." The first task, not an easy one, is to translate the word *praeis*. Ulrich Luz wrote, "The understanding of the beatitude of the *praeis* is made extraordinarily difficult by the semantic open-endedness of this word."[22] The singular *praus* is an adjective meaning "amiable, peaceful, gentle, lowly, meek, humble." A man who is *praus* or a woman who is *praeia* are the opposites of someone who is rough, harsh, violent, irritable, aggressive and quarrelsome. *Prautes*—meekness—is the virtue of humble goodness that is at the opposite extreme from anger and violence.

This beatitude, with no parallel in the macarisms of Luke, has a clear connection with Psalm 37. According to the Greek translation of the Septuagint, the tenth verse of this psalm reads: *Hoi de praeis klēronomēsousin gēn* ("but the *praeis* will inherit the earth"). Behind the word *praeis* of this Greek translation we find, in the original Hebrew, the term *anawim*, which is usually translated into Greek by *ptōchoi*, the "poor" of the first beatitude. The third beatitude is thus an echo of the first, insisting on one particular implication of the first and most basic macarism.

As is almost always the case when the New Testament alludes to the Old, it is useful to examine the full context of the

[22] U. Luz, *Matthew 1–7: A Commentary*, 236.

quotation. Since the New Testament authors were very familiar with the Old, when they refer to it they hope that, in the mind of the reader, there will be an echo not just of the few words that they quote explicitly, but of the entire passage where these are found. Psalm 37 says:

> Do not fret because of the wicked;
>> do not be envious of wrongdoers,
> for they will soon fade like the grass,
>> and wither like the green herb.
>
> Trust in the LORD, and do good;
>> so you will live in the land, and enjoy security.
> Take delight in the LORD,
>> and he will give you the desires of your heart.
>
> Commit your way to the LORD;
>> trust in him, and he will act.
> He will make your vindication shine like the light,
>> and the justice of your cause like the noonday.
>
> Be still before the LORD, and wait patiently for him;
>> do not fret over those who prosper in their way,
> over those who carry out evil devices.
>
> Refrain from anger, and forsake wrath.
>> Do not fret—it leads only to evil.
> For the wicked shall be cut off,
>> but those who wait for the LORD shall inherit the land.
>
> Yet a little while, and the wicked will be no more;
>> though you look diligently for their place, they will not
>>> be there.
> *But the meek* [anawim/praeis] *shall inherit the land,*
>> and delight themselves in abundant prosperity.
>
> (Ps 37:1-11, NRSV; italics mine)[23]

[23] New Revised Standard Version Bible, National Council of the Churches of Christ, New York 1989.

The author of the psalm is speaking to a person of integrity who is disturbed by the apparent success of violence: the wicked receive what they desire and those who break the law seem to triumph. The psalmist asks the believer to be patient; the violent will not have the last word. The third beatitude thus emphasizes a virtue that has to accompany poverty in spirit: the ability to control one's anger, to resist patiently the seduction of violence, which appears to be a rapid solution to oppression and injustice. This "patient resistance" (in Greek, *hypomonē*) is not the apathy of someone who does not care about injustice, but the force necessary to resist the temptation of using the same weapons as the violent to combat them.

The poor in spirit have to train themselves to be masters of the art of non-violence, to the point of acquiring a virtue that causes them to resemble God himself, who never imposes himself by force or ceases to love. This is certainly not a facile love; it can even seem superhuman, but it is a road that is possible, taken not just by Jesus but by other men and women who have tried to struggle for justice without hatred.[24]

---

[24] We find a significant witness to this in the words spoken by Martin Luther King in a famous sermon, rhetorically aimed at the enemies of emancipation: "We shall match your capacity to inflict suffering by our capacity to endure suffering. We will meet your physical force with soul force. Do to us what you will and we will still love you. We cannot in all good conscience obey your unjust laws and abide by the unjust system, because non-cooperation with evil is as much a moral obligation as is cooperation with good, and so throw us in jail and we will still love you. Bomb our homes and threaten our children, and, as difficult as it is, we will still love you. Send your hooded perpetrators of violence into our communities at the midnight hour and drag us out on some wayside road and leave us half-dead as you beat us, and we will still love you. Send your propaganda agents around the country, and make it appear that we are not fit, culturally and otherwise, for integration, and we'll still love you. But be assured that we'll wear you down by our capacity to suffer, and one day we will win our freedom. We will not only win freedom for ourselves; we will so appeal to your heart and conscience that we will win you in the process, and our victory will be a double

The third beatitude does not call us to a meekness understood as indolence or submission; it aims at the formation of people who have so much love and resilience that they are able to "overcome evil with good" (Rom 12:21). The good news of this macarism is that violence will not have the last word in history, but that men and women conformed to the image of Christ, "gentle (*praus*) and humble of heart" (Matt 11:29), will be able to transform the world. They will be the ones who will "inherit the earth."

Happy Those Who Hunger and Thirst for What Is Right

In Luke, Jesus calls happy "those who are hungry now." This beatitude is another reiteration of the first macarism, with God's preferential love for the poor taking concrete shape in those who suffer from the consequences of dire poverty. Matthew's version, however, emphasizes a moral virtue, because the hunger and thirst spoken of are not for bread, but for justice.

Justice or righteousness (*dikaiosyne* in the original)[25] was one of the fundamental virtues for the Greeks. A just or righteous (*dikaios*) man was someone able to behave fairly with his fellows and with the *polis* as a whole. In the New Testament, however, this term should be understood "as a concept of relationship, which was shaped in a peculiar way in the Old

---

victory." *The Papers of Martin Luther King, Jr.*, IV: Symbol of the Movement, January 1957–December 1958, Berkeley 2000, 341–342.

[25] Translator's note: in English translations of the Bible, the Greek word *dikaiosyne*, "justice" in the classical texts, is usually translated instead as "righteousness." To English-language ears, the former translation risks emphasizing too much the legal and political dimensions of the notion, whereas "righteousness" could seem to be merely an inner state or an attitude limited to private life; moreover, the word is scarcely ever used any more outside of the Bible. Perhaps the best solution is to paraphrase *dikaiosyne* as "what is right."

Testament and Jewish tradition."[26] For the authors of both the Old and New Testament, then, justice is the correct manner to be in relationship with God and with others.

The history of the people of Israel witnesses again and again to the fact that justice is rooted in a right relationship with God. Its starting-point is the initiative taken by the Lord in establishing a covenant with a particular nation; beginning from this axiom, the faithful realize that to be just or righteous means to respond to the Lord's free choice, "loving him with all your heart, with all your soul and with all your strength" (Deut 6:5). This right relationship with God is the basis of the mutual respect between the members of the community. Justice comes from heaven—it is a divine initiative—but it must be lived out on earth, as these poetic verses of Isaiah express:

> Drip, o heavens, from above;
> let the clouds rain down justice (*tsedeq*).
> Let the ground open
> and bud forth salvation and righteousness (*tsedeqah*).[27]

This special friendship with God, reserved at one time to a single nation, is now offered through Jesus to every human being. The imminence of the Kingdom opens a new possibility of communion with God and makes possible new relationships among human beings, enabling us to envisage an end to violence, the domination of some over others, and a climate of mistrust. The Sermon on the Mount is the offer of this new righteousness, greater than that of the scribes and Pharisees (Matt 5:20).

Almost two thousand years ago Jesus, by calling the hungry happy, revealed himself as a kind of visionary of our time. With this beatitude he declared that non-conformity is a virtue

[26] K. Kertelge, *Dikaiosynē*, in H. Balz – G. Schneider (eds.), *Exegetical Dictionary of the New Testament*, Grand Rapids 1990, I, 326.
[27] Isaiah 45:8. This verse is attributed to Second Isaiah.

proper to his followers in the realm of interpersonal relations. Anyone who longs for justice in the world experiences something very similar to those who are hungry and thirsty. To them all, Jesus promises the good fortune of being filled (*chortasthēsontai*). It is true that perfect justice will only be possible in the new creation, beyond this world; it is possible, however, to begin building it today. Being a Christian means participating in Jesus's program to extend friendship to all throughout the earth. To persevere in this task a person has to acquire the "unsettled" attitude of hunger and thirst for justice, which begins with the development of a sensibility able to perceive the great suffering that there is in the world because of the unjust system of relations. It is not enough to weep with those who weep—the theme of the second beatitude—it is necessary to examine whether this weeping is the result of injustice and, when this is the case, to rebel against it without falling into the temptation of violence—the theme of the third beatitude.

It is hard not to abandon, in the course of one's life, a true non-conformity against the way that this world functions; it requires the perseverance that comes by forming a habit. The person who is happy in the style of the Beatitudes refuses to settle down in a well-being limited to just a few people and commits herself not to give up until there is true justice for all, not, obviously, in a theoretical sense, through mere words, but by means of a lifestyle that becomes a way of being, a virtue.

Happy the Merciful

This beatitude begins a series of three that have no parallels in the macarisms of Luke's gospel. They all emphasize activities characteristic of the Christian community, which configure a form of being in the persons who practice them. Being merciful, pure of heart and a peacemaker is inseparable from the concrete practices through which these virtues gradually become our second nature.

Jesus declares "happy the merciful, for they will obtain mercy" (*makarioi hoi eleēmones, hoti autoi eleēthēsontai*). The merciful person (*eleēmōn*) is someone who, moved by a feeling of compassion for the suffering of another person, acts to relieve that suffering. In the original context in which the Beatitudes were proclaimed, the essential work of mercy was almsgiving. In fact, the English word "alms" is derived from the Greek term for mercy, *eleēmosynē*.

Giving money to someone in need is, in many situations, an effective way to help them, but there are other ways too. The tradition of the church has elaborated a double list of the works of mercy. Seven are corporal: to feed the hungry, to give drink to the thirsty, to clothe the naked, to visit the sick, to free the captive, to shelter the traveler and to bury the dead;[28] and seven are spiritual: to instruct the ignorant, to counsel the doubtful, to admonish the sinner, to forgive offenses willingly, to comfort the afflicted, to bear wrongs patiently, to pray for the living and the dead. Today this double list could be extended and adapted: to defend the rights of the most vulnerable, to offer legal aid to "illegal" migrants, to collect funds for the construction of schools in developing countries, to denounce the abuse of a minor, etc. In any event, to be merciful is inseparable from acting compassionately towards those who suffer.

Like the other beatitudes, this macarism has an eschatological dimension. The reward promised to the merciful consists precisely in "receiving mercy," an expression that in the original corresponds to a single word, *eleēthēsontai*. The form of this verb is what grammarians of New Testament Greek call a divine passive: the unmentioned actor is God, who will accord mercy to those who, during their lives, have been merciful. In the final judgment, even the best human being will

---

[28] The six first ones are inspired by Matthew 25:31-46. The seventh comes from the good works of Tobit (Tob 1:16-20).

need God's compassion. Those who have practiced mercy on earth with their fellows will then receive it from the Lord. It is not necessary to wait until the end of time, however, to begin to participate in the happiness promised to this beatitude.

A virtue expresses a personality trait of a happy human being. And no one can be happier than a person who comes close to God's own way of being. In Luke's gospel we read, "Be merciful as your Father is merciful" (Luke 6:36).[29] Acquiring this virtue makes us resemble God's way of being.

Theologians have not been very interested in mercy as a quality of God. In fact, "in the traditional as well as in the more recent dogmatic handbooks, God's mercy is treated only as one of God's attributes among others. Most often it is treated only briefly and then only after the attributes that derive from God's metaphysical essence."[30] Both in the past as well as today, theology has been concerned more about categories like God's infinity, eternity, omnipresence, omniscience and omnipotence rather than reflecting on God's mercy. And yet, this is one of the qualities of the Lord emphasized most strongly in the Bible.

In the Old Testament, the concept of mercy is expressed mainly by means of two words: *rahamim* and *hesed*. The first comes from the noun *rehem*, which in Hebrew refers to the womb. God has a maternal aspect, showing tenderness and care to the faithful like that of a mother for her child. The second term, *hesed*, describes a grace that overflows all human expectations concerning God's assumption of our constitutive neediness.[31]

[29] Luke uses a synonym of *eleēmones, oiktirmones*.
[30] W. Kasper, *Mercy: The Essence of the Gospel and the Key to Christian Life*, New York 2014, 9–10.
[31] "To think that God, who is all-powerful and holy, concerns himself with the distressing and self-caused situation of human beings, that God see the wretchedness of poor and miserable people, that he hears their lament, that he bends down in condescension, that he descends to persons in their need and, despite every human infidelity, concerns himself

Although it is true that some passages of the Old Testament portray a God who is vindictive and strict, the biblical tradition taken as a whole, even before Christ, gives greater weight to the image of a merciful God, "slow to anger and overflowing with *hesed*" (Ps 145:8), a God who takes the initiative to assist wretched human beings and is quick to offer his forgiveness. On the basis of this image of God in the Jewish tradition, Jesus draws a portrait of the merciful God in his parables—the father of the prodigal son, the shepherd seeking the lost sheep, the woman looking for a lost coin—but above all he shows God's compassion through his own activity towards the sick and with sinners.

James Keenan has defined mercy as "the willingness to enter into the chaos of persons in their need and, despite every human infidelity, concerns himself with them again and again, and that he forgives them and gives them another chance, even though they had another."[32] It is thus precisely our God who agreed to enter into this confused disorder that is human history in order to offer salvation to us. Believing in such a God has moral consequences, since Christians should try to emulate God in this character trait so characteristic of him. The movement goes from faith to morality, from the contemplation of God to the activity that seeks to imitate him. On the other hand, we can also follow this road by going in the other direction: whoever practices mercy is transformed, and by acquiring this virtue becomes more able to contemplate God as he is. A "virtuous circle" is thus created between faith and practice, through which believers become more similar to their Lord.

---

with them again and again, and that he forgives them and gives them another chance, even though they had deserved just punishment—all of this exceeds normal human experience and expectation; all of this transcends human imagination and thought." Ibid., 43.

[32] J. J. Keenan, *Moral Wisdom: Lessons and Texts from the Catholic Tradition*, Lanham 2010, 118.

Happy the Pure in Heart

Purity is one of the most universal religious and moral categories.[33] In the most varied cultural and religious systems there exist persons, things or actions that are considered *impure*: forbidden foods that cannot be eaten, "dirty" actions—many related to sexuality—that must not be committed, castes of "untouchables" who have to be avoided, etc. The norms that establish what is pure and what is impure and dictate the rituals of purification for what has been contaminated vary according to beliefs, but the concern to avoid impurity transcends all creeds and religions.

The British anthropologist Mary Douglas, in the 1960s, offered an interesting theory to explain the vast phenomenon of purity. The root of her interpretation is the intuitive observation that impurity is "matter out of place"[34] Objects are not pure or impure in themselves, but rather with reference to an order: mud is not dirty when it is in a field, but it is when *out of place*, on the floor of an apartment, for example. It is not inappropriate to wear a bathing suit on the beach, but it is in a formal gathering. Tomato sauce is perfectly pure on spaghetti but dirty when it spots a white shirt.

> [Dirt] implies two conditions: a set of ordered relations and a contravention of that order. Dirt then, is never a unique, isolated event. Where there is dirt there is system. Dirt is the by-product of a systematic ordering and classification of matter, in so far as ordering involves rejecting inappropriate elements.[35]

[33] Paul Ricoeur speaks of the "stain" as a "pre-ethical" universal symbol that manifests the fear of suffering that can be felt by someone who transgresses an order. *Finitude and Guilt*, Washington DC 1965.

[34] M. Douglas, *Purity and Danger: An Analysis of Concepts of Pollution and Taboo*, London 1966, 2001, 36.

[35] Ibid.

The society in which Jesus lived was obsessed with purity. There were forbidden foods, like pork or shellfish; other foods, lawful in themselves, could become impure if mixed (such as meat and milk products); those who touched a corpse or a menstruating woman had to purify themselves if they wanted to return to normal, etc. All these norms helped to consolidate a system in which "everything was in its place." A certain order is necessary in order to live, but we must not forget the dark side of every system of purity: the mental barriers it creates also cause divisions between human beings, dividing society into the healthy and the ill, the good and the wicked, compatriots and foreigners.

By his words and especially by his actions, Jesus attacked the system of purity, since it was part of his project to cross the boundaries erected by the obsession of his contemporaries in order to encounter the excluded. And so we see him letting lepers touch him and sitting at table with sinners.

According to the logic of purity, a clean person had to avoid contact with the unclean so as not to be contaminated by their uncleanness. Jesus reverses the process: the purity in him cleanses the sick, restoring their health and rescuing them from being outcasts. This happened when a woman who was bleeding touched him, a woman who was not only sick but also impure, because she was in a constant state of menstruation. When she entered into contact with Jesus, instead of contaminating the Master, she was "contaminated" by the cleansing power that radiated from him (Mark 5:25-34).

The beatitude of purity of heart must be understood in the context of this attitude of Jesus in opposition to the system of purity. One day, some Pharisees and teachers of the law questioned Christ about the behavior of his followers, who were disregarding the norms of washing their hands before meals. In this context, Jesus proposed this teaching to his disciples:

> Are you still so unintelligent? Don't you realize that everything that goes into the mouth goes down into the belly and then out to the latrine? But what comes out of the mouth

comes from the heart, and that is what makes a person unclean. For from the heart come evil thoughts, murder, adultery, fornication, theft, false witness and slander. That is what makes a person unclean; eating without washing one's hands does not make anyone unclean.[36]

In this passage, Jesus excludes as irrelevant any impurity that comes from without; what really matters is impurity that comes from the heart. A long list of acts against one's neighbors illustrates what evil intentions can lead to: murder, adultery, fornication, theft, false testimonies and slander. In this way, Jesus of Nazareth confronts the norms of purity prevailing in the religious world of his time with what he calls "purity of heart."

Purity of heart is contrasted with the way the Pharisees understood purity and also with the perception of the clean and the unclean discovered by Mary Douglas in many cultural systems, since it is not based on an order that classifies things and divides people into exclusive groups. It goes in the exact opposite direction: the purity that Jesus recommends is an impulse of the heart to do good, which is able to leap over the mental barriers created by systems of purity.

It is no accident that the reward promised to the pure of heart is the vision of God. The ability to see correctly is one of the fundamental themes of the Sermon on the Mount. During this discourse, Jesus says:

[36] Matt 15:16-20. Cf. Matt 15:1-20 // Mark 7:1-23. Both Mark and Matthew transmit the teaching of Jesus that what enters through the mouth is not a cause of impurity; what comes out of the heart is. But they reach different conclusions regarding the import of these words. Mark comments: "Thus he [Jesus] declared all foods clean" (Mark 7:19). This evangelist, writing for Christians from a pagan background, interprets the words of Jesus as a declaration that abolishes the norms of *kosher* dietary restrictions. Matthew, whose community is Jewish-Christian, does not go that far. For him, what Jesus declares as unnecessary is only to wash one's hands before meals, a Pharisaic custom that the Law of Moses did not require of all the Jews.

> The eye is the lamp of the body. If your eye is simple (*haplous*),[37] your whole body will be in the light. But if your eye is evil (*ponēros*), then your whole body will be in the dark. And if the light in you is darkness, how dark will you be! (Matt 6:22-23)

This saying is found in a section of the Sermon on the Mount that brings together various teachings of Jesus against avarice (Matt 6:19-24). The sentence contrasts the simple (*haplous*) eye, able to perceive the light found in every creature, to the diseased (*poneros*) eye that distorts and obscures reality. The name of this sickness is *avarice*. The greedy person lives a dark life, because he or she is governed by the logic of scarcity. Such people think: "There is not enough for everybody; I have to accumulate, so that others do not appropriate what I need to be happy."

Jesus teaches us that, if we know how to look, we will discover in the world the overabundance of God: "Consider carefully (*emblepsate*) the birds in the sky; they do not sow or reap or gather their crops into storehouses, and yet your heavenly Father feeds them" (Matt 6:26). God has created a world in which there are possibilities of fullness for all, since he has even adorned the wild flowers with magnificence (Matt 6:25-34). All we have to do is to liberate our goodness of heart and leap over the walls erected by the system of purity to discover that God did not create the borders or the laws of property. "In the world there is more than enough for the needs of all, but not enough for the greed of some" (Gandhi).

The clean of heart "will see God." This statement has an eschatological dimension that refers to the vision of God when the Kingdom comes in fullness, but the Kingdom is already

[37] Some English versions of the Bible translate *haplous* as "healthy." The word does not mean "healthy," however, but rather "simple, not double." Cf. T. Schramm, *haplous*, H. Balz – G. Schneider (eds.), *Exegetical Dictionary of the New Testament*, I, 123.

breaking into history. With a heart liberated from the fear of being contaminated, with eyes purified from avarice, it is possible already to see the overabundant gift of redemption.

Happy the Peacemakers

In this macarism, the virtue and the practice that lead to peace converge. Behind the expression "peacemakers" there is a single Greek word, *eirēnopoioi*, from *eirēnē* (peace) and the verb *poieō* (to make, to do). The *eirēnopoios* is the person who has the virtue of creating peace around him- or herself, but this virtue, like every virtue, can only be acquired by practicing it. Peacemakers are women or men who work for peace and who have made this work so much a part of their being that it has become one of their character traits.

The psalmist urges us to "turn from evil and do good; seek peace and pursue it" (Ps 34:14). Peacemaking is a fundamental characteristic of the spirituality of the Old Testament. This search should not be understood as a facile irenicism limited to soothing souls and avoiding conflict. The Hebrew word for peace, *shalom*, comes from the Semitic root *slm*, which means "to have enough"; but it is a term that, far from indicating a mere sufficiency, points towards a state of plenitude and abundance; *shalom* "indicates everything that constitutes healthy, harmonious life, the full development of the powers of the healthy psyche."[38]

It is clear that peace/*shalom* does not refer to the mere absence of conflict, nor to the maintenance of the status quo by means of the threat of force. Pope Paul VI referred to it when he stated: "When we fight poverty and oppose the unfair conditions of the present, we are not just promoting human well-being; we are also furthering man's spiritual and moral development, and hence we are benefiting the whole human

---

[38] G. Gerleman, *slm*, in E. Jenni – C. Westermann (eds.), *Theological Lexicon of the Old Testament*, Peabody 1997, III, 1339.

race. For peace is not simply the absence of warfare, based on a precarious balance of power; it is fashioned by efforts directed day after day towards the establishment of the ordered universe willed by God, with a more perfect form of justice among men."[39]

When Jesus spoke of the Kingdom, he proclaimed this peace that is coming into the world as God's definitive gift to humanity. The peace of the Kingdom, however, implies a task: the followers of Christ, who have been reconciled to God through Jesus, have the duty to place themselves at the service of God's plan of universal reconciliation (2 Cor 5:18).

Peacemakers receive the promise to "be called children of God." The connection between working for peace and being God's sons and daughters is not evident, but if we keep on reading the Sermon on the Mount, only a few verses later we find these words that explain what it means to be children of God:

> You have heard that it was said: Love your neighbor and hate your enemy. But I say to you: Love your enemies and pray for those who persecute you. In that way you will be sons and daughters of your heavenly Father, because he causes the sun to rise on both the wicked and the good, and sends rain upon the righteous and the unrighteous. For if you only love those who love you, what reward will you have? Do not tax-collectors do the same? And if you are friendly only to your relatives, what are you doing that is so extraordinary? Do not pagans do the same? You must be perfect, as your heavenly Father is perfect. (Mt 5:43-47)

It is obvious that working for peace involves creating harmonious relationships between the members of the Christian community. And yet it cannot be limited to the inner life of the group of believers.[40] To be truly a son or daughter of God we

---

[39] Paul VI, Encyclical *Populorum progressio*, 76.
[40] U. Luz, *Matthew 1–7: A Commentary*, 241.

have to go beyond the circle of those who maintain relations of trust and reciprocity among themselves. We have to imitate God our Father, who makes his sun rise upon the good and the wicked, and even go to the point of "loving our enemies." Creating peace/*shalom* is not something that is kept within the walls of one's own group; it must be extended to all, including those who, in whatever way, try to hurt us.

This task requires a special kind of person, with an unusual audacity animated by the hunger for justice as well as formed in the arts of non-violence and mercy. That this macarism concerning peacemakers is found almost at the end of the list of beatitudes can be a way of indicating that the six virtues previously mentioned have to culminate in effective work for peace.

Some commentators have seen an ironic resonance in the seventh beatitude.[41] At the time when Matthew was writing his gospel, the theme of the *pax romana* was an important aspect of imperial propaganda. According to the official account, the first emperor, Octavius Augustus, had brought peace to the vast territories controlled by the Romans in an unprecedented historical undertaking. Octavius and his successors were hailed as "builders of peace" and "sons of the gods."[42] The Christians, however, remained critical regarding this "peace" acquired by military victories and maintained through the terror inspired by the legions. The *shalom* that Christ came to bring is the fruit of harmony and human development. That peace is not imposed from above; it is built from below, when men and women who are poor in spirit commit themselves to putting their lives at the service of others, with mercy and with pure hearts.

---

[41] H. D. Betz – A. Y. Collins, *The Sermon on the Mount*, 138.

[42] One of the places where this conjuncture between the divine nature of the emperors and their title as peacemakers is most clearly visible is in coinage. The coins in circulation were an excellent means of propaganda for the Empire. Many of them depicted the figure of the divinized emperor and inscriptions alluding to peace. Cf. F. A. Muñoz, *La pax romana*, in F. Muñoz – B. Molina (eds.), *Cosmovisiones de paz en el Mediterráneo antiguo y medieval*, Granada 1998, 221–222.

Happy Those Persecuted for What Is Right

Those persecuted for what is right (*hoi dediōgmenoi hekenen dikaiosynēs*) are promised the same thing as the poor in spirit: "the Kingdom of heaven belongs to them" (*autōn estin hē basileia ton ouranōn*). With this reference to the first beatitude, the eighth and last macarism of Matthew recapitulates the series: if poverty in spirit is the virtue that opens the gates of the Kingdom, persecution for the sake of justice is the culmination. The promise attached to this beatitude repeats the first in the present indicative: the Kingdom of heaven already belongs to those who suffer persecution.

What is specific to this beatitude is that it is followed by a long gloss in which the discourse abandons the third-person plural of the previous macarisms. Jesus, speaking here in the second person, does not only address the characters in the story who are listening to his Sermon on the Mount, but also the persecuted Christians who read the gospel. In this way, he emphasizes that this beatitude applies to all: "Happy are you when people insult you and persecute you and say all manner of evil things [falsely] against you because of me" (Matt 5:11).

On the other hand, this final macarism, unlike the others, does not describe a virtue. Being persecuted is not a character trait that can be cultivated, but an external situation that goes against our will. This beatitude does not add a virtue to those indicated in the seven previous ones, but it proclaims happy those who meet with difficulties in their search for justice.

Many New Testament texts state that the followers of Jesus will be persecuted. In addition to the martyrs who gave their lives for their faith during the first centuries, daily persecution was more subtle and insidious: from difficulties with non-Christian family members and the exclusion from certain groups and civic associations, to insults by neighbors and harassment from the authorities. Living the justice of the Kingdom was costly.

This macarism emphasizes the fact that whoever wants to experience the happiness of the Beatitudes will have to get used to living against the stream and will have to assume, as the price to pay, the mocking laughter of neighbors and threats from the civil authorities. Moreover, they will have to learn to discover in persecution the means to grow as believers. In this sense, persecution is revealed as the adequate ecosystem for maturing the virtues listed in the Beatitudes. These virtues are not acquired by the comfort of a life without contradictions, but in the struggle against the temptation of abandoning the road and becoming like everyone else.

"Be glad and overjoyed" (*chairete kai agalliasthe*), says Jesus to those early Christians and to all those who have come afterwards. To be glad (*chairō*) refers to an inner emotion, being overjoyed (*agalliaō*) to the noisy manifestation of the exhilaration we feel. The Beatitudes thus conclude on this intense note of rejoicing: "Be glad and overjoyed, because your reward is great in heaven; in the same way they persecuted the prophets before you" (Matt 5:12).

All who set out on the road of the justice of the Kingdom and let themselves be molded by the virtues of the Beatitudes are part of a story that is greater than their own lives. Still more, they are situated in the wake of the prophets of past centuries and oriented towards a future in which the eternal light of the Kingdom will be manifested, but without forgetting that this joyfulness is already accessible in the present, here and now.

A Happiness in the Style of Jesus

Matthew's Beatitudes list seven virtues that draw a portrait of the happy person in the style of Jesus. They are "a sort of veiled interior biography of Jesus, a kind of portrait of his figure"; precisely because they have been fully realized in Christ, "they are directions for discipleship."[43]

---

[43] Benedict XVI, *Jesus of Nazareth: From the Baptism in the Jordan to the Transfiguration*, London 2007, 74.

The Beatitudes mark out a path; they list forms of training we have to undertake in order to reach fulfillment. The first of them opens the door to all the others: poverty in spirit. Recognizing that we are fragile and by this awareness opening ourselves to God gives us access to the Kingdom here and now. We protect ourselves from life by seeking security in material wealth or in experiences that produce the illusion of having Paradise under our control, but these are only illusions that distance us from the truth of what we are. The first beatitude awakens us from this dream and makes us realize that, beneath the disguises with which we cover our nudity, there is a body beloved by God. And we discover in a new way that all of us, as human beings, are equal in our radical neediness. All those who suffer are my brothers or sisters, and whatever makes me indifferent to them distances me from my own truth and from God. The good news is that, outside of the dark cave that represents the fear of not being worthy of love, the sun of God's Kingdom is shining.

The three beatitudes that follow the first are reflections of it. The second defends the audacity to weep, invites us to recognize our suffering and exhorts us to learn to express it before others. This beatitude calls us to create social spaces where it is acceptable to say: "I am not doing well," and to form communities where people can share their difficulties in order to receive true counsel.

The third beatitude recalls the virtue of non-violence. It is not enough to have warm homes in which to share our feelings. It is promised to whoever wishes to live the happiness of the Beatitudes that they will "inherit the earth." Let us aspire to transform this world, dominated by violence, without reproducing in the process the same relationships of submission that today humiliate the poor and make creativity impossible. Inheriting the earth does not mean gaining power. The virtue of non-violence is made up of a resistance that never gives up until it exhausts evil by doing good.

Remaining hungry is the fourth beatitude. It becomes concrete by our remaining nonconformists in the face of a world where suffering is in great measure the result of hardness of heart and human stupidity. The poor in spirit must learn to weep with those who weep, but they also have to ask themselves about the causes of suffering and not accept the condition of our world as an immutable reality. To change it they will not use violence, but learn to satisfy their hunger for justice by putting into practice—as many Christians have done throughout history—projects that alleviate suffering and cause peace to flourish.

The beatitude of mercy leads to a second triad of virtues concerning essential practices. Aristotle imagined God as an impassible being, happy in the eternal contemplation of himself. If God is God, he thought, why would he be interested in anything outside of the eternal perfection that he is? But the God who revealed himself in Jesus is moved by the suffering of his creatures. Learning to be merciful has, as one of its two faces, being moved inwardly at the pain of others, and as its second to find remedies for evil by means of concrete acts. Learning to be merciful is an education of the sentiments that refines our ability to perceive the suffering of others. It is, in addition, an eminently practical training, because it is only by doing works of mercy that we become merciful, and in this way we can become more and more like this mysterious God who has chosen to enter into our chaos.

Purity of heart subverts the different forms of purity that divide humanity into separate groups. Our secularized society has rejected traditional forms of purity, but it maintains systems of segregation. Around the rich countries fences are built—and not just metaphorical ones—that separate them from the outcasts of the South. Behind this wall, the rules are more subtle: whoever does not bear the signs of triumph bears the stigma of the impure. Purity of heart means leaping over those walls, letting loose the Good Samaritan that we all have within us and liberating the kindness of heart that does not differentiate races and classes.

The seventh beatitude brings the list to a climax in the word peace/*shalom*. In the biblical tradition, this peace is not seen as the absence of conflicts, but as life lived to the full. The mature Christian is a peacemaker because for him or her peace is a true virtue. Building peace with the means of peace is the work of each person, but also and above all the task of a community formed to be "a city set on a hill." The reason the church exists is to be the sign and instrument of a peace based on justice, made possible by the inbreaking of the Kingdom.

These seven virtues that model Christians in the image of Jesus require living a life that goes against the stream, and this will never be easy. The New Testament authors assure us, as a result of their own experience, that those who dare to live in this way will encounter persecution. The Gospel tells us that the gate to this happiness is narrow, but it also assures us that it is possible to pass through it, because it has been opened once and for all by the example of the One who gave his life for our liberation (cf. Matt 7:13; Mark 10:45; John 13:1). Being happy means acquiring these virtues and coming to be like Jesus.

CHAPTER SIX

Love

Three Words to Express Love

There are several different words in Greek that can be translated into English by the word "love." Here, to describe Christian love, we will select three: *eros*, *philia* and *agapē*. Each has its own characteristics.

The term *eros* refers to that mysterious force that draws us out of ourselves and leads us to seek the loved one and be united with him or her. Plato reflected on this kind of love in his dialogue, the *Symposium*. During an evening of feasting washed down with good wine—the Greek word *symposion* means "a gathering of drinkers"—a group of friends discourse on *eros*. One of them, the comic writer Aristophanes, recalls for the others the myth of the "spherical human beings."[1] In ancient times—*fabula*—there existed three types of human beings: masculine, feminine and androgynous. All of them were round and were complete beings. As a punishment of the gods, each of them was divided in two: the masculine being produced two men; the feminine, two women; the androgynous, a man and a woman. The men and women of today, according to this myth, are incomplete beings who long for what they once were. For this reason, men and women who

---

[1] Plato, *Symposium*, 190–192.

came from the androgynous being search for members of the opposite sex, whereas men who came from the primordial masculine being and women who came from the primordial feminine being are attracted by those of the same sex.

This explanation of *eros* as a natural impulse to completion is one of the most famous discourses of the *Symposium*, even if it is not the only one we find in that treatise. Other guests describe *eros* as the force of attraction exercised upon us by something that is beautiful (*kalon*). Beauty has a power that calls us out of ourselves; sexual attraction is only a particular case of this universal impulse. Plato continues his reflection defending as the highest expression of *eros* the search for beauty in its pure form, and he concludes that the supreme manifestation of *eros* consists in love for ideas and souls.[2]

In speaking of love Aristotle employs the term *philia*, which we translate as friendship-love. *Philia* is distinguished from *eros* in that it is not a force that draws us out of ourselves, but a free relationship that must be consciously cultivated. Two individuals are *philoi*, "friends," when each one seeks the good and the happiness of the other. For Aristotle, happiness is the goal of a process by which we mold our personality according to those indicators of human excellence that are the virtues. But virtues can only be acquired through practices that suppose a social setting or context. Such a context is, for Aristotle, the Greek city-state (*polis*), in which the citizens participate in its government and functioning.[3] For example, by behaving courageously in the defense of the *polis*, every citizen acquires the virtue of courage, and by exercising prudence in taking decisions in the assembly (*ekklēsia*), everyone becomes prudent. This *philia* or friendship-love is, for the philosopher, something that links the citizens together, so that in seeking

[2] *To ep'eiden kalon* ("the beautiful as form or idea"), 210b.

[3] A citizen is "he who has right to share in deliberative or juridical authority" (*exousia koinōnein archēs bouleutikēs ē kritikēs*), Aristotle, *Politics*, III, 1, 1275b17.

the common good they learn to appreciate one another and stimulate one another to give the best of themselves.

At the same time, such a friendship is only possible when the city is able to propose common ends that allow the efforts of all to converge. The *philia* Aristotle speaks about is not a desire that attracts one person to another because he or she is beautiful (*eros*), but one that connects and unites those facing the same direction. Loving others as friends means esteeming them and helping them give the best of themselves as we work together in a project that is beyond us both. This love presupposes a reciprocal relationship: I also desire and hope that you want my good and stimulate me to be better.

The term *agapē* is the preferred word in the New Testament to speak of "love." This Greek word, scarcely used outside of the world of the Bible, was popular among New Testament writers because it was employed in the Septuagint, the Greek version of the Old Testament used by the early Christians.[4] Why the translators of the Septuagint preferred to use *agapē* is a question debated by the specialists. Some suggest that it was due to a distant phonetic resemblance to the Hebrew *ahabah*, which means "love." Others, however, point out that by preferring a term not very common in everyday usage, the authors of the Septuagint wanted to distinguish the love that is spoken about in the sacred texts from the *eros* or *philia* characteristic of Hellenistic culture.[5]

In any case, in the New Testament the word *eros* is not found even once, but the term *philia* is used with a certain frequency,

---

[4] The verb *agapaō* appears 266 times in the Septuagint, compared to 15 occurrences of *phileō*. Similarly, *agapaō* is found 143 times in the New Testament, while *phileō* only 25. In the New Testament, the noun *agapē* is found 116 times, and the adjective *agapētos* (beloved) 61. *Philos* (friend) is found on 23 occasions, while *philia* (friendship) only once (Jas 4:4). All these statistics can be found in G. Schneider, *agapē*, in H. Balz – G. Schneider (eds.), *Exegetical Dictionary of the New Testament*, Grand Rapids 1990, I, 8–12.

[5] W. Günther – H-G. Link, "Love," in C. Brown (ed.), *The New International Dictionary of the New Testament Theology*, Exeter 1978, II, 538–547.

and when it is used, its meaning coincides with *agapē*.[6] In this way, although *agapē* retains a certain religious aura that comes from its preferential use in the Septuagint, it functions basically as a synonym of *philia*, because both words name a love that consists in seeking the good of the other and that requires a personal decision; for this reason it is distinguished from *eros*, which acts as a force that draws me out of myself.[7]

When the Bible was translated into Latin, the word *caritas* was chosen to translate *agapē* and *amicitia* as the equivalent of *philia*. But although caritas became the specifically Christian form of love, the most clear-sighted theologians understood that between *amicitia* and *caritas* there was a basic equivalence. Thomas Aquinas, for instance, affirmed in his *Summa theologiae* that "*caritas est amicitia.*"[8] This does not mean, of course, that Aristotle's teaching about friendship coincides with the Christian doctrine of love, but that between both nouns there is an affinity that makes it possible to grasp the first starting from the second. It is not a coincidence that both the Aristotelian *philia* and the New Testament *agapē* refer to a love that consists in the conscious and deliberate search for the good of the other, that builds us up as persons in the context of a shared social project. For Aristotle, this project was the *polis*; for Christians, the Kingdom of God.

The Twofold Commandment of Love

It would be hard to find anyone who would argue against the central importance of love in Christian theology and ethics. For this reason, it is striking that Jesus almost never speaks of love in the gospels of Mark, Luke and Matthew, which are

[6] A very revealing passage of this equivalency is the dialogue between Peter and the risen Jesus in John 21:5. Cf. R. Schnackenburg, *The Gospel according to Saint John*, New York 1982, III, 362–363.

[7] Benedict XVI offers a masterful commentary of the meanings of *agapē* and *eros* in the first part of his encyclical *Deus caritas est*, and shows their complementarity.

[8] Thomas Aquinas, *Summa theologiae*, II–II, q. 23.

precisely the ones that, according to the exegetes, communicate his words with the greatest accuracy. This scarcity of explicit references to love does not mean, of course, that it was not an important topic for Jesus; in fact, each and every one of his actions during his life can be explained as expressions of love. Perhaps it was for this reason that Jesus did not constantly have this word on his lips.[9]

Given that the reflections of Jesus about love that we have are few and far between, the *logion* known as the twofold commandment of love appears especially significant. In this famous statement, transmitted by the three synoptic gospels, the Master recalls the central place occupied by love in religious and moral life:

> One of the scribes asked him, "What is the most important commandment?" Jesus replied, "The most important is: *Listen, Israel, the Lord our God is the only Lord. You shall love the Lord your God with all your heart and all your soul and all your mind and all your strength.* The second is this: *You shall love your neighbor as yourself.* There is no other commandment greater than these." (Mark 12:28-31 // Matt 22:34-40 and Luke 10:25-28)

A scribe (*grammateus*) asked Jesus a question that appertained to the erudite discussion concerning which, among the many precepts of Judaism, was the most important. Jesus answered in the purest rabbinical style by juxtaposing two separate sentences of the Torah taken from the books of Deuteronomy (6:4-5) and Leviticus (19:18b). Later on, rabbis would

---

[9] Another important saying about love is "love your enemies," transmitted by Q (Matt 5:44 // Luke 6:27). The Golden Rule is sometimes quoted among the commandments to love, but strictly speaking it does not command us to love. In any case, this saying is not original with Jesus. In John's gospel, Jesus speaks more often about love, but these discourses appear to be constructions of the Johannine community rather than *logia* of the Master. Cf. J. P. Meier, *A Marginal Jew: Rethinking Historical Jesus*, IV, Law and Love, New Haven 2009, 478–576.

call this hermeneutic technique *gezera shawah*; it consisted in connecting two separate passages of Scripture that contain a word in common in order to interpret them both.[10] Jesus obviously knew the Law well and the exegetical methods used to interpret it.

Some authors have made an exhaustive examination of the Old Testament and the Jewish literature prior to and contemporary with Jesus in order to demonstrate the originality of this sentence: no one else, as far as we know, had connected those two passages of the Law in the way that Jesus did.[11] In any event, the relationship between the idea of love towards God and towards human beings is a familiar theme in the Old Testament (cf., for example, Hos 12:7; Mic 6:8; and Ps 15:2-5).

Among the Jews who were contemporaries of Jesus, Philo (c. 20 BCE–c. 50 CE) is the one who is closest to him in the formulation of this doctrine. In his work *On the Decalogue*, this Alexandrian scholar affirms that people who want to reach perfect virtue must be both friends of God (*philotheoi*) and friends of human beings (*philanthropoi*).[12] The idea that love for God and for one's neighbor is the culmination of the Law thus seems a natural conclusion in the evolution of the best Jewish thinking of the first century.[13]

---

[10] B. D. Chilton, "Rabbinic Rules of Interpretation," in S. E. Porter (ed.), *Dictionary of Biblical Criticism and Interpretation*, New York 2007, 304.

[11] Concerning the historicity of this passage, cf. J. P. Meier, *A Marginal Jew*, IV, 484–528.

[12] Philo of Alexandria, *On the Decalogue*, XXII, 110.

[13] The Talmud transmits a curious anecdote that also expresses the idea that love for God and for one's neighbor sums up the entire Law: "On another occasion, it happened that a certain pagan came to Shammai and said to him, 'I will become a proselyte on the condition that you can teach me the entire Torah while I am standing on one foot.' Shammai threw him out with a builder's ruler that he held in his hand. Then the man went to Hillel, who said to him, 'What you do not want for yourself, do not do to your neighbor. That is the whole Torah; the rest is commentary. Go and learn.'" Babylonian Talmud, *Shabbath*, 31a. Although the anecdote is attributed to Hillel and Shammai, who lived around the time of Christ,

Mark's gospel implicitly recognizes the relationship of the twofold commandment of love to the moral reflection of contemporary Judaism when it shows the scribe welcoming favorably Jesus's reply:

> The scribe said to him, "Very good, Teacher. You are right to say that God is one and there is no other alongside him; and to love him with one's whole heart and one's whole mind and one's whole strength, and to love one's neighbor as oneself, is more important than all the burnt-offerings and sacrifices." Jesus, seeing that he had answered wisely, said to him, "You are not far from the Kingdom of God." (Mark 12:32-34)

Luke takes a further step concerning the idea of the closeness of the twofold commandment of love to the Jewish tradition.[14] In his version, an expert in the Law (*nomikos*) asks Jesus, "What must I do to inherit eternal life?" Jesus answers his question with another question: "What is written in the Law? How do you construe it?" (Luke 10:25-26). According to Luke, it is the expert in the Law himself who answers with the words of the twofold commandment that Mark places on Jesus's lips.[15] If we accept, with most exegetes, that Luke is copying and editing Mark, we can appreciate the bold commentary he makes on his predecessor. Loving God and one's neighbor is a principle perfectly within the scope of traditional Judaism,

---

the Babylonian Talmud is a work composed between the third and sixth centuries CE. This story is probably much later than the composition of the New Testament.

[14] Matthew's version is similar to Mark's, although Jesus speaks with a Pharisee and not an expert in the Law. Moreover, while in Matthew and Mark the episode concerning the main commandment takes place in Jerusalem during the last week of Jesus's life, in Luke it occurs at the beginning of his journey to Jerusalem.

[15] It was probably Luke who united the episode concerning the main commandment, which came from Mark, with the parable of the Good Samaritan, which he knew from a separate source. Cf. J. A. Fitzmeyer, *The Gospel according to Luke X–XXIV*, New York 1985, 882–883.

so that what Jesus came to bring was something more. To find this "something more," all we need to do is to keep on reading: the lawyer, "wishing to justify himself, asked Jesus, 'And who is my neighbor (*plēsion*)?' " (Luke 10:29).

In Greek, *plēsion* means "someone near," and in the text quoted from Leviticus it translates the word *re'a*. This Hebrew term does not have a universal meaning; it designates "a co-participant in the cultic community of Israel . . . the adult male who has full citizenship in the people of Israel."[16] Even some Jewish groups of the time, such as the Essenes of Qumran, limited the number of those who could be considered neighbors to members of their own sect. The expert in the Law, consequently, is asking Jesus about the extension of the commandment to love: Who am I obliged to love and who is exempt? He asks Jesus to limit the circle that separates a neighbor from someone who is not.

Jesus's reply to this second question is one of his best-known parables: the Good Samaritan. On the road from Jerusalem down to Jericho, a man falls into the hands of bandits who leave him half dead. A while later, first a priest and then a Levite pass by without helping him. Finally, a Samaritan has compassion on him: he takes care of him, puts him on his mount and brings him to an inn where he can recover. The provocation of the parable lies in that fact that a Samaritan is made the hero of the story, because Jews and Samaritans hated one another ferociously.[17]

---

[16] M. Ebersohn, *Das Nächstenliebegebot in der synoptischen Tradition*, Marburg 1993, 41–42.

[17] Although the beliefs of the two religious groups were fairly similar—both believed in the one God YHWH and considered the Torah as God's revealed Word—they differed in their conviction concerning where to worship God. While the Jews believed that the Temple of Jerusalem was the only place where legitimate sacrifices could be offered, the Samaritans challenged this belief by offering them in their Temple on Mount Garizim. Since the exile in Babylonia, the Samaritans had been opposed to the restoration of Jerusalem, even helping the Syrians in the second century BCE in their war against the Jews. The Jews, for their part, attacked and

When he ended his story, Jesus asked his hearer, "Which of the three, in your opinion, became (*gegonenai*) a neighbor to the man who fell into the hands of the bandits?" Note that the verb "to be" (*eimi*) of the lawyer's question is changed on the lips of Jesus to the verb "to become" (*gignomai*). The question "Who is my neighbor?" is transformed into "Who became a neighbor?" Christ challenges with this parable the static notion of neighbor that the lawyer's question presupposes. My neighbor is not someone who *is*, but who *becomes*: it is a choice that arises from mercy and that transforms us. "My neighbor is someone who needs me and whom I can assist."[18] By choosing the most improbable of the characters—a Samaritan—to incarnate the pole of the one who showed compassion and became a neighbor, Jesus invites the listener to be open to surprises.

Jesus's last phrase, "Go and do the same," clearly shows the ethical intention of this exemplary story. The reader is invited to identify himself with the Samaritan and to act as he did. We discover in this way a characteristic of Christian *agapē* that distinguishes it both from the Aristotelian *philia* as well as from other forms of love that are shared in family, religious, national or political circles and that understand love as something that we only owe to "our own." Christian love does not limit itself to seeking the good of those close to us by nature: the God of Jesus always invites us to widen our horizons.

Welcoming the Stranger

Like the Samaritan in the story, Jesus is remembered as someone who "went about doing good" (Acts 10:38). For him, loving was more an activity than a discourse. Examining all

---

burned the Samaritan temple in the year 128 BCE. R. E. Brown, *The Gospel according to Saint John I–XII*, New York 1966, 170. Beginning in the first century CE, some Samaritans infiltrated the temple of Jerusalem and scattered human bones to render it impure, thus preventing the Passover celebration that year from taking place. Flavius Josephus, *Jewish Antiquities*, 18.2.2.

[18] Benedict XVI, *Deus caritas est*, 15.

the activities that Jesus accomplished and that expressed his love would go beyond the limits of our investigation, so we will concentrate on *hospitality*, a practice that cemented the community that he himself founded.

The author of the Letter to the Hebrews writes: "Abide in brotherly love (*philadelphia*); do not neglect hospitality (*philoxenia*); by means of it, some have welcomed angels without realizing it" (Heb 13:1-2). Christians have to treat the brothers and sisters who make up the Christian community with love—*philadelphia* comes from *phil-*, "love," and *adelphos*, "brother"—but Christian love cannot be limited to those within the group. And so, the letter then exhorts believers to cultivate hospitality (*philoxenia*), which comes from *phil-*, "love," and *xenos*, "stranger."[19]

This New Testament text is referring to a passage from the book of Genesis in which Abraham welcomes into his tent three unknown men, who turn out to be angels (Gen 18:1-16). In the heat of the day, explains the story, the patriarch was seated at the entrance to his tent, near the oak of Mambre. Three men approach him. When he sees them, Abraham runs to receive them, asks them to accept his hospitality and offers them water to wash their feet. Then he tells his wife to prepare bread, while he sacrifices a calf, "tender and fattened," to prepare a banquet. When he departs, the mysterious guest—now the text refers in the singular to what earlier had been described as three visitors—promises, "I will surely return to you a year from now and your wife Sarah will have a son." That son will be named Isaac, and he will provide continuity to the promise made by God to Abraham, that he would have descendants "as numerous as the stars in the sky or the grains of sand on the seashore" (Gen 22:17).[20]

---

[19] The opposite of this word is sadly familiar to us: *xenophobia*, fear or hatred of strangers.

[20] The beautiful icon of Andrej Rublev (1360–1430), entitled "the Trinity," represents, according to a patristic interpretation of Genesis 18, the theophany of the triune God.

This story shows that from the beginning of salvation history an intimate link existed between hospitality and blessing. Whoever welcomes a stranger is blessed by God.[21]

The institution of hospitality is common to many ancient and modern peoples and cultures across the world. In the cultures around Israel, offering hospitality was considered a sacred duty.[22] It was the responsibility of the head of the family or clan to decide whether to offer hospitality to a wayfarer who was passing through his territory. If the stranger accepted it, a special relationship was formed between both parties during the agreed time of his stay. It was customary for the guest not to ask for anything, but the host had to offer the best of his home to honor him. In exchange, it was expected that the guest would bring news of the lands he had passed through and tell stories of his native country. People were appreciative when the person welcomed showed his satisfaction and gratefulness upon leaving, as well as his blessing according to the generosity of the treatment he received. The protection of the guest from all danger was one of the most sacrosanct obligations; in some biblical texts, people even sacrifice the security of the members of their own family to defend a guest.[23]

To understand the meaning and the significance of this practice, we must realize the extreme vulnerability of travelers in the ancient world. In our time, visiting other countries is

[21] Other significant texts on hospitality in the Old Testament: Gen 19:1-14; 24:1-67; Exod 2:15-22; Deut 24:1-22; Josh 2:1-24; Judg 4:17-22; 6:11-24; 13:1-25; 19:1-10; 19:11-30; 1 Kgs 17:7-16; 2 Kgs 4:8-17; Ruth 2:14-16; Tob 7:1-17.

[22] Bob Stallman, after studying the welcome of strangers in ancient Sumerian, Akkadian, Egyptian, Hittite and Ugaritic texts, affirms that the practice of hospitality in Israel "does not appear to differ significantly from what we know of social customs throughout the ancient Near East." *Divine Hospitality in the Pentateuch: A Metaphorical Perspective on God as Host*, Philadelphia 1999, 160.

[23] As in Gen 19:1-8 and Judg 19:11-24. Cf. V. H. Matthews, "Hospitality and Hostility in Genesis 19 and Judges 19," *Biblical Theology Bulletin* 22 (1992), 13–15.

considered something enjoyable, but in those days people did not travel for pleasure: leaving one's own region was an extremely risky business. The dangers were not only plentiful outside of inhabited areas, where there were no police forces to ensure order, but also within those areas, since the stranger was at the mercy of the local residents, who could apply the laws as they wished.

The ancient wisdom of hospitality perceived, in this vulnerability, possibilities for a mutually enriching exchange. While the visitor depended upon the inhabitants for his basic necessities—food, shelter, protection, etc.—he also had something valuable to offer: information about faraway places, useful knowledge from other cultures, and exotic gifts. The traveler was also bearer of "goods" that were even more precious: his stories could stimulate an imagination weary of listening to the same things over and over; his customs, so different, had the possibility of revealing the finitude and relativity of the locals' own vision of life; his visit made it possible for his hosts to open themselves to new horizons of understanding.[24] In this way, the fear inspired by the unknown and the possible threat represented by the stranger were transformed, thanks to the act of hospitality, into an opportunity for broadening people's lives; in addition, the gladness of the feast with which his visit was celebrated gave free rein to the joy of discovering more life in life, breaking the circle of provincialism that weakens the perception of reality.

In this sense the practice of hospitality, offered and received, brought the people of Israel to a deeper understanding of their God. And so, in the story of Abraham and the angels, the reader who has faith can discover the presence of the deity in the passing strangers;[25] not for nothing is God the Other with a capital O, whose "very epiphany consists in soliciting us by

[24] T. W. Ogletree, *Hospitality to the Stranger: Dimensions of Moral Understanding*, Philadelphia 2004, 1–3.
[25] The intuition that the stranger can be a god in disguise is also found in Homer, *Odyssey* 17, 485–487.

his destitution in the face of the Stranger, the widow and the orphan."[26] Hospitality is thus the exercise of letting others lead me to widen the limits of my reality and to dispose myself to be open to the One who throws into disarray all our preconceived notions—God.

We know that Jesus made hospitality the key to his mission. Mark writes:

> He called the Twelve to him and began to send them out by twos, giving them authority over evil spirits. He ordered them not to take anything for the road except a staff. No bread, no pouch, no money in their wallets. They were to wear sandals, but not take two tunics. And he told them, "Whenever you enter a house, stay there until you leave the place. If they do not receive you or listen to you in a place, leave them and shake the dust from the soles of your feet as a witness against them." (Mark 6:7-11)

Matthew and Luke offer parallel passages, with a few differences (Matt 10:5-15; Luke 9:1-16). In these texts, Jesus requires his disciples even to forsake sandals and a staff, things allowed by Mark.[27] The most notable difference, however, is that in Matthew and Luke the instructions by Jesus of what the disciples should do in the houses that welcome them are much more detailed (Matt 10:12-14; Luke 9:4; 10:8-9). In Luke, there is even a second sending that is even more numerous, involving seventy-two disciples (Luke 10:1-16).[28]

[26] E. Levinas, *Totality and Infinity*, Pittsburgh 1995, 78.

[27] In both Luke and Matthew, they are told not to take a staff. In Matthew, but not in Luke, the use of sandals is also prohibited. Cf. Mark 6:8–9; Matt 10:9–10; Luke 9:3.

[28] Some of the oldest manuscripts that we have speak of seventy disciples, and others of seventy-two. The experts in textual criticism are divided concerning which of the two expressions could be original; many think that there are no sufficient reasons to opt for one or the other of the two variations. Cf. B. M. Metzger, *A Textual Commentary on the Greek New Testament*, Peabody MA 2006, 150–151.

Most New Testament scholars assume that this tradition, common to Matthew and Luke and absent in Mark, comes from a hypothetical text that is generally known as "Q." Comparing the material common to Matthew and Luke permits the reconstruction of the words of Jesus that such a document would have presumably recorded.

> "Into whatever house you enter, first say: Peace to this house! And if a son of peace be there, let your peace be there, let your peace come upon him; but if not, let your peace return upon you. And at that house remain, eating and drinking whatever they provide, for the worker is worthy of one's reward. Do not move around from house to house. And whatever town you enter and they take you in eat what is set before you. And cure the sick there, and say to them: The kingdom of God has reached unto you."[29]

These words contain precise instructions on what the disciples should do in the homes that offer them hospitality, namely: bless the residents by wishing peace for them, sharing their meals, healing the sick and proclaiming that the Kingdom is at hand. For this mission, sharing room and board is not a mere optional circumstance, but the outward sign of a communion that is at the heart of Jesus's project. Through hospitality, both the hosts and the visitors can have an experience of the Kingdom; in sharing, the Kingdom begins to become concrete as a form of life, and not only as a small group of radical followers who have left everything, but also for a wider circle, those who open their homes and their lives to give shelter to the bearers of the Good News. In this regard, Jesus said, "Whoever gives even a cup of cold water to one of these little ones because he is my disciple will not lose his reward" (Matt 10:42; cf. Mark 9:41).

---

[29] J. M. Robinson – P. Hoffmann – J. S. Kloppenborg (eds.), *The Critical Edition of Q*, Minneapolis 2000, 166–175.

The Reign of God does not force itself on anyone; for this reason, it is important that those sent—*apostoloi* in the Greek original—present themselves without the self-sufficiency that having one's own resources makes possible. Jesus sends them out with "no bread, no pouch, no money in their wallets." In this way they will depend totally on the people of goodwill who accept to offer them hospitality. The command not to bring a staff, an instrument which, in addition to helping someone to walk, was used as a weapon for self-defense, reinforces the vulnerability of these travelers, so that the proclamation of the Kingdom is in the hands of those who are not able to impose themselves by their power or dazzle by their intellectual superiority: it is offered in the fragility of some travelers needing to be welcomed.

The missions of the Twelve and the seventy-two disciples, narrated in the Synoptic Gospels, witness to how Jesus shared with his disciples the mission of proclaiming the Reign of God. One of the consequences of this activity was the creation, already during Christ's life, of a network of families linked to his movement,[30] since some of those who welcomed the missionaries and their announcement continued a relationship with Jesus and his disciples. We do not know how many families were involved in this way, but we know the names of some of the hosts: the house of Peter's family in Capharnaum, where his mother-in-law lived (Mark 1:29-30); the house of Simon the leper, in Bethany, where Jesus spent the night during his visits to Jerusalem (Matt 21:17; 26:6; Mark 11:11-12; 14:3); and equally in Bethany, the house of Lazarus and his sisters Martha and Mary, who, according to John the evangelist, were friends of Jesus (John 11:1-44).[31]

We do not know a lot about what happened to the families linked to the Jesus movement after his death. What we do

---

[30] S. Guijarro, "The Family in the Jesus Movement," *Biblical Theology Bulletin* 34 (2004), 119.

[31] Martha and Mary also appear in Luke 10:38-42.

know, thanks to the letters of Paul and the Acts of the Apostles, is that the missionary strategy consisting in the creation of a network of homes linked by the comings and goings of itinerant missionaries was continued by the first Christians after Easter. Different New Testament passages allow us to know the names and the profiles of some of the heads of those households. The book of Acts speaks of Cornelius, a Roman centurion who resided at Caesarea Maritima, the port city of Judea. This official was a "godfearer," in other words a man of pagan background who believed in the one God of Israel. After offering hospitality to Peter in his home, he asked to be baptized with his family (Acts 10:1-48).

A few chapters later, at the beginning of Paul's mission to Greece, in Philippi we meet Lydia, a merchant dealing in purple cloth. She too, after hearing Paul's preaching, was baptized with the members of her household and offered hospitality to the apostle (Acts 16:14-40).

Another woman, Phoebe, appears as the person in charge (*diakonos*) of a Christian community that met in her house at Cenchreae, a few kilometers from Corinth. In the Letter to the Romans, Paul calls her a "benefactor" (*prostatis*), in other words, someone who helped him with her financial resources and with her hospitality (Rom 16:1).

Moreover, we know the names of several itinerant missionaries. Following the Lord's command, they normally traveled in pairs (Mark 6:7; Luke 10:1). Paul formed a team at the beginning of his apostolate with Barnabas,[32] but afterwards we see him in the company of Timothy and Silas, among others.[33] In his First Letter to the Corinthians, he tells us that Peter traveled with his wife (1 Cor 9:5); from this verse we can understand that it was normal for these missionary couples to be husband and wife. We have the names of some of them: Priscilla and

---

[32] Acts 13:1-2, 7, 43, 46, 50; 14:12, 14, 20; 15:2, 12, 22, 25, 35-36, 39.

[33] Acts 16:1; 17:14-15; 18:5; 19:22; 20:4; Rom 16:21; 1 Cor 4:17; 16:10; 2 Cor 1:1, 19; Phil 1:1; 2:19; Col 1:1; 1 Thess 1:1; 3:2, 6; 2 Thess 1:1.

Aquila, Jewish exiles from Rome who, like Paul, were tent-makers;[34] Andronicus and Junia, "compatriots and fellow-prisoners, well-known among the apostles" (Rom 16:7).

A first approximation to Christian homes and the missionaries they welcomed with their hospitality attests to the leading role of certain women;[35] this is surprising, given the strongly patriarchal character of Greco-Roman society. In addition, the fact that female itinerant missionaries could exist, and that one at least was given the title of *apostle*,[36] is significant. There is no reason to think that they accompanied their husbands merely as spouses, since the texts allow us to understand that they took an active part in the task of announcing the Gospel.[37]

Another interesting fact is the elevated social position of some of the heads of these households. Pauline Christianity was an interclass movement, insofar as people of different social ranks were part of it.[38] It was important for the mission to find at least one house large enough in every locality to welcome the itinerant missionaries who passed through and the community that regularly met there.

Archeological studies show that the typical house in the Roman Empire in the first and second centuries of the Common Era was built around two patios.[39] This design created a semi-public space around the outer patio, where the head of the household received his guests, and a private space around

[34] Acts 18:2, 18, 26; cf. 1 Cor 16:19 and Rom 16:3.

[35] B. Thurston, *Women in the New Testament*, New York 1998, 30; cf. A. de Mingo Kaminouchi, "San Pablo y las mujeres," *Moralia* 26 (2003), 7–29.

[36] We refer to Junia, mentioned in Romans 16:7. This title may have been applied as well to other women, such as Prisca, for example.

[37] J. Cook, "I Cor 9:5: The Women of the Apostles," *Biblica* 89 (2008) 352–368.

[38] R. Aguirre, *Del movimiento de Jesús a la Iglesia cristiana*, Bilbao 1987, 102. Cf. W. A. Meeks, *The First Urban Christians*, New Haven 1983, 51–73.

[39] Cf. J. González Echegaray, "Reflexiones sobre la Domus-Ecclesia del siglo I," in G. Hernández Peludo – S. Guijarro Oporto (eds.), *Los ecos de la Escritura: Homenaje a José Manuel Sánchez Caro*, Estella 2011, 119–151.

the inner patio reserved for family members. The outer patio, normally surrounded on four sides by a two-story construction, formed an enclosure perfectly adapted to the meetings of the Christian community. This kind of house also had enough rooms to welcome the itinerant missionaries. The owners of such buildings were obviously individuals with economic resources. It is very possible that, in many cases, these men and women exercised the leadership of the assembly (*ekklēsia*) that met in their homes.[40]

Hospitality thus became the practice that sustained this new network of human relationships that came to be called "the church." In the Letter to the Ephesians, an epistle that is usually considered deutero-Pauline, in other words written not by Paul but by disciples of his from a later generation, the term *ekklēsia* has already acquired the meaning that it has today, that of a universal institution; nevertheless, in the letters written by Paul himself it designates a concrete assembly of Christians that meets in one place. The *domus ecclesiae*, the house of a Christian family that opened its home to welcome the members of the local community and the itinerant missionaries, was the meeting-place that made this new social reality possible.

After the Edict of Milan in the year 313, with the construction of temples and basilicas and the consequent abandon of the church model based on the *domus ecclesiae*, the form of hospitality that characterized pre-Constantinian Christianity was coming to an end. Still, in the course of the following centuries hospitality was reborn in new contexts. Monastic life, which would characterize the development of Christendom during the Middle Ages, gave great importance to hospitality. The Rule of Saint Benedict, for example, ordered that guests be received as Christ himself, and gave the abbot himself the task of welcoming them. The monks had to wash the

---

[40] Cf. L. W. Countryman, *The Rich Christians in the Church of the Early Empire: Contradictions and Accommodations*, New York 1980.

feet of the visitors and take care of their needs, both spiritual and material.[41]

Pilgrimages were another of the practices that kept hospitality alive. Welcoming pilgrims became one of the works of mercy. For not only were places of welcome set up, but the first hospitals in Europe were established to take care of pilgrims who fell ill. In our day, in countries that receive migrants, Christian groups have organized themselves to welcome large numbers of men and women who arrive as political refugees or seekers of employment. Attentiveness to their needs and the struggle for their rights are renewing this age-old practice.

In one of his most influential works, *The Meaning of Christian Brotherhood*, Joseph Ratzinger defended "the formation of a definite, tangible brotherly community." In his opinion, what distinguishes the brotherhood of Christians from the universal fraternity promoted by the Enlightenment (the *fraternité* of the French revolution) is that the church has shown throughout its history that only by living fraternity in a concrete fashion can we avoid "the empty romanticism" of the Enlightenment proposal or any other one based on mere theory.[42] A thesis found throughout the book is that, in order for the Christian community not to dissipate into mere fantasy, it is important to set the limits that enable someone to decide whether he or she belongs to the community or not, "for brotherhood, extended so far, becomes unrealistic and meaningless."[43] In the final pages of the book, Ratzinger shows how these limits are not exclusive, but are at the service of communicating the concrete and real love that exists in the community to the entire human family.

[41] Cf. *The Rule of Saint Benedict*; chapter 53 concerns the reception of guests.
[42] J. Ratzinger, *The Meaning of Christian Brotherhood*, San Francisco 1993, 70; the book was written in 1960.
[43] Ibid., 16.

Hospitality (*philoxenia*) presupposes *philadelphia*, the brotherly love that becomes concrete in the Christian community equipped with certain limits, but at the same time it challenges those limits. It is clear that no hospitality would be possible without a real community that welcomes, but that community would not be Christian if it did not cultivate the widening proper to *agapē*, which opens the circle of closeness to accommodate the *xenos*, the one who is different, the other. Communities open to *philoxenia* were the nodes that knitted together the network of relationships that began to call itself "the church." Despite the profound transformations of the Constantinian era, hospitality did not cease to emerge in every historical period. This constant creativity confirms that without *philoxenia*, the *philadelphia* of Christians runs the great risk of withdrawing into a self-referential outlook.

Sharing the Lord's Supper

The first Christians met, welcoming one another in their homes, to celebrate the Lord's Supper. Those communities, brought together in the name of Christ Jesus, experienced his presence and shared the certainty that he was alive. This Lord, the conqueror of death, impelled them to create a new social reality on earth as the first-fruits of the new human relationships established by the inbreaking of the Reign of God.

The Bible does not offer a handbook on how to celebrate the Eucharist, since the authors of the New Testament put their trust in a living Tradition. Still more, when the church speaks of Tradition, she is thinking above all of this rite that has been kept alive and is transmitted by the celebration itself. In fact, those who take part again and again in the Mystery of the bread shared and the wine poured out are transformed by the way of thinking, feeling and living of Christ, who gives himself.

In every culture, meals in common constitute a moment when bonds are created and when what the community considers the attainment of happiness, of the "good life, is expressed."[44] The table setting, the mutual recognition of sitting down together, the sharing of food and the conversation that accompanies it do not only forge links between the participants but also show what they are and what they are becoming together; they witness to the image of a well-being that goes far beyond the satisfaction of the needs of each individual. A banquet is the staging of the shared happiness that we call *the common good*.

Jesus was especially sensitive to this possibility of the table as a means to express his Gospel. Near the beginning of Mark's account, Christ calls Levi, a tax-collector, who responds immediately and leaves his work to follow him.[45] Then, Jesus and his followers go to his house to eat. The evangelist informs us that "many tax-collectors and sinners were at table with Jesus and his disciples" (Mark 2:15). In a society of that nature, obsessed with purity, eating with "sinners" and people who were considered unclean was a serious transgression. The Pharisees were scandalized that Jesus accepted "tax-collectors and sinners" in his company, whereas for him, eating with the excluded formed an essential part of the Gospel. His open meals, in the company of those rejected by society, were an act that showed better than any words that all without exception were invited into the Kingdom of God.

The four gospels consider that the multiplication of the loaves and fishes represented a crucial moment in the mission of Jesus.[46] Isaiah had prophesied, as one of the signs that God's Reign was beginning, that God himself "will make for all peoples on this mountain a banquet of rich foods, a banquet

[44] *Euzoia*, "the good life," is one of the synonyms that Aristotle uses for *eudaimonia*.

[45] Mark 2:15-17 // Matt 9:10-13 // Luke 5:29-32. In Matthew's gospel, the protagonist of the scene is called Matthew instead of Levi; cf. Luke 15:2; 19:7.

[46] Mark and Matthew each tell of two feedings: Mark 6:30-44 and 8:1-10; Matt 14:13-21 and 15:32-39. Luke and John only tell of one: Luke 9:10-17 and John 6:1-14.

of fine wines, rich foods and choice wines" (Isa 25:6). Jesus decided to actualize here and now this great meal marking the inbreaking of the Kingdom, without waiting for later, and he did it with great simplicity. In the accounts of the feeding of the multitude, there is no talk of expensive wines or fancy food, but only bread and fish, and a large crowd of hungry people. The guests do not sit at elegant tables; green grass is enough for their tablecloth. This is Jesus's style: to accomplish messianic acts using simple elements.[47]

In the account of the feeding of the multitude, to speak of what Jesus does with the bread, Mark uses the same verbs he will use to describe the Last Supper. In both passages Jesus, taking (*labōn*) bread, says the blessing (*eulogēsen*), breaks it (*kateklasen/eklasen*) and gives it (*edoken*);[48] for the evangelist it is thus obvious that this miracle prefigures the Eucharist that his community will celebrate as the memorial of the Last Supper. Every time Christians celebrate the Lord's Supper, they make present the banquet of the last days. In this way, believers in the Risen Christ anticipate the end (*eschaton*) that will mark the goal (*telos*) for which the human race was created—to be united with the Lord in a great feast, a banquet of communion.

The Last Supper cannot be understood if it is disconnected from the other meals of Jesus. The table shared with sinners, the multiplication of the bread and fishes, and the other references to banquets and feasts that we find in the life of Christ

---

[47] In Mark, a few chapters previously, Jesus had restored the twelve tribes of Israel—one of the tasks of the Messiah—by naming twelve men, fishermen and ordinary people, as his apostles (Mark 3:13-19). Later on he will enter Jerusalem as the Messiah on a donkey (Mark 11:1-11) and will purify the Temple symbolically with a whip made of ropes (Mark 11:1-19).

[48] Mark 6:41 // 14:22. The verbs also coincide, in the second version of Mark (8:6), with the sole difference that *eulogēsen*, "to bless," is replaced by *eucharistēsas*, "to give thanks." The accounts of the Last Supper in Luke 22:19 and 1 Cor 11:24 use the same verbs as this second multiplication, the only variant being the omission of the verb "to give" in Paul's letter.

and in his parables reveal the character of a man who, when he was faced with an imminent death, wanted to come together with his friends around a table.

In a context marked by the celebration of the Jewish Passover, Jesus, recognizing the closeness of his death, met with his disciples for a special meal where he shared bread and wine with them.[49] It was typical of him to perform acts of great transcendence with ordinary means; in this case, he attempted to show his disciples the meaning of his death: "And while they were eating he took bread, said the blessing, broke it and gave it to them saying, 'Take it; this is my body'" (Mark 14:22). His body, broken like the bread, will hang on the cross; this life shared and given will be nourishment for his followers.

According to the three Synoptic Gospels, the cup passed from hand to hand during that banquet was the seal of a new covenant, which brought into being a new people. The project of the Kingdom, for which Jesus gave his life, did not cease with the Master's death, because a community of men and women would continue his activity. The evangelist Luke introduces into the account of the Last Supper words about *power and service* (Mark and Matthew situate them at the end of the section of the journey up to Jerusalem) in order to emphasize that what characterizes this new community is to be a bearer of this power-and-service of God revealed in Jesus:

[49] Both John and the Synoptics agree that the Last Supper took place the night before his crucifixion, which happened on a Friday. That Friday was, for John, the fourteenth day of the month of Nisan and, according to the Synoptics, the fifteenth. The difference is of great importance, because the fifteenth of Nisan was the Jewish Passover, and the meal celebrated on the previous evening was the Passover meal. According to the Synoptics, the Last Supper was a Passover celebration, whereas for John it was not. Bible scholars have tried to reconcile both contradictory testimonies. They propose, for example, that in the Judaism of the time there were alternative calendars to the official one, such as that used by the Essenes. According to this conjecture, John would be describing a Passover meal celebrated on another day. In any case, the climate of those days in Jerusalem marked both versions of the Last Supper.

> The greatest among you must be as the least, and the leader
> as the one who serves. For who is greater, the one sitting at
> table or the one who serves? Is it not the one sitting at table?
> But I am in your midst as the one who serves. You are the
> ones who have remained with me in my trials, and I have
> designated you to rule as my Father designated me to rule.
> (Luke 22:26-29)[50]

The Fourth Gospel distances itself from the synoptic account: it does not relate the words and actions over the bread
and wine during the Last Supper, nor does it make any reference to sayings about power and service. We know that the
absence of the words of the institution is not due in John to an
ignorance of the tradition of the Lord's Supper, because this
gospel expresses, in more radical terms, faith in the presence
of Christ in the Eucharistic bread and wine (cf. John 6:53). In
any case, for some reason John has replaced the account of the
institution of the Eucharist with that of the washing of the
disciples' feet. This is how the Fourth Gospel expresses in an
original fashion the same intuition the Synoptics insist upon:
at the Last Supper, Jesus made manifest the meaning of his
death as an act of supreme service that was the culmination
of a life of self-giving, a life for others. In addition, by ordering
the disciples to live with this same attitude, Jesus laid the foundations of a new community based on a surprising practice of
authority (John 13:12-15).

The words and actions of Jesus would have remained merely
beautiful wishes for a better world had he not returned from
the dead. The Kingdom is not a *utopia*, because it has a "*topos*,"
a place in this world where it has already come about—the
risen Body of Christ.[51] Several of the appearances of the Risen

---

[50] Cf. Luke 22:24-30; Matt 20:25-27; Mark 10:42-45.

[51] "Utopia" is a word coined by Thomas More (1478–1535) as the title
of one of his most famous books. It is composed of the terms *ou* ("no")
and *topos* ("place"). Utopia describes the organization of an ideal society,
but it does not really exist anywhere.

Christ recounted by Luke and John as well as in the so-called "longer ending of Mark"[52] occur during a meal.[53] In these accounts, the experience of the community that assiduously celebrates the Eucharist is superimposed on the recollection of the post-paschal encounters with the Lord.

Week after week, believers in the Risen Christ gathered to remember Jesus, performing the same actions and repeating the same words as he did at the Last Supper. In doing so, they experienced his real presence in their midst. Still more, it was his presence in that shared meal that sustained them. That act became the center of their lives and transformed them. A new human community was taking shape around those tables.

The texts that recall the Last Supper in the Synoptic Gospels are the Scriptural basis of the institution of the Eucharist, but they do not describe how the rite was performed. In the New Testament, only one passage presents, with a minimum of details, the way the Lord's Supper was celebrated, namely 1 Corinthians 11:17-34. On the other hand, realizing that the apostle Paul wrote his First Letter to the Corinthians probably around the year 56, this text is the oldest testimony we have concerning it.

All the letters of Paul except the Letter to the Romans were sent to communities founded by the apostle himself. Through these missives, which were read aloud in the assembly, Paul exercised his responsibility of instructing these communities when it was not possible for him to visit them. Paul deals with practical problems in his epistles; he is not interested in pure theoretical speculation, but neither is he interested in offering

---

[52] In the oldest manuscripts, Mark ends with 16:9. In the first nine verses of chapter 16, Mary Magdalene and Mary, the mother of James and Salomé, find the tomb empty and hear the announcement of the resurrection, but no appearance of the Risen Christ is mentioned. Mark 16:9-20 is known as the "canonical ending" or the "longer ending" of Mark. There is a widespread consensus among the experts in textual criticism that it is a later addition to the original text.

[53] Luke 24:30-32, 41-43; John 21:1-15; Mark 16:14; cf. Acts 10:41.

recipes or rules for conduct. What Paul does is a particular kind of *moral theology*: he shows how wrong behavior is the tip of the iceberg of deeper maladjustments and he reflects theologically about them.

In his First Letter to the Corinthians, Paul responds to community conflicts that he heard about through information received from some of the members.[54] In 1 Corinthians 11–14 he deals with questions related to the order of the weekly meetings; more specifically, in 11:17-34 he tackles a problem that took place during the celebration of the Eucharist. The text begins in this way: "In giving you instructions I do not praise you, because your meetings are not profitable but rather detrimental. For above all, I hear that when you meet together in community (*ekklēsia*) there are divisions (*schismata*) among you, and in part I believe it" (1 Cor 11:17-18).[55]

But in what exactly did these divisions consist?[56] Verses 20-22 sketch a profile of the situation: "When you meet, it is not to eat the Lord's Supper. For when it is time to eat each takes their own supper, and one goes hungry while another gets drunk. Don't you have homes to eat and drink in? Or do you have contempt for the assembly (*ekklēsia*) of God? What can I say to you? Praise you? In this I cannot praise you!" (1 Cor 11:20-22).

---

[54] His informers were, among others, "Chloe's people" (1 Cor 1:11) and "Stephanas, Fortunatus and Achaicus" (1 Cor 16:17).

[55] The expression "in part I believe it" belongs to a rhetorical strategy of false incredulity. The context makes it clear that Paul believes the reports that he has received. His pretended incredulity serves to further emphasize to his readers his amazement and anger. Cfr. M. M. Mitchell, *Paul and the Rhetoric of Reconciliation: An Exegetical Investigation of the Language and Composition of 1 Corinthians*, Tübingen 1991, 153.

[56] I follow the opinion of Gerd Theissen, which enjoys a good reception by the specialists. Cf. "Social Integration and Sacramental Activity: An Analysis of 1 Cor 11:17–34," in *The Social Setting of Pauline Christianity: Essays on Corinth*, Edinburgh 1982. Cf. J. D. G. Dunn, *The Theology of Paul the Apostle*, Grand Rapids 1998, 609.

The weekly meetings of the Christians were held in people's homes, when possible in a large house belonging to a rich Christian. A cultural difference between us and the ancient Romans is that, for them, to be busy was not a sign of social prestige; the Greco-Roman elite openly despised work. A well-to-do man took care of his business in the morning; to do so in the afternoon was looked down upon. As a result, wealthy and idle people could enjoy the luxury of coming to the community supper on time, because they had no obligations. The same was not true of the poorer people, who had to finish their chores before coming to the meeting. We can imagine the scene in this way:

> We meet in the outer patio of a Roman house. In the room specially prepared for banquets, called *triclinium*, at one end of the patio, the patricians of the house gather, surrounded by some friends from the same social class. They have been there for over an hour and have polished off the most appetizing delicacies. Gradually other men and women begin to arrive. Their dress shows their lesser rank. They take their places in the rooms that open on to the patio and take part in the feast. Others follow; when they arrive, there is only room on the pavement of the patio, and almost nothing to eat or drink. At that moment, the one presiding at the celebration says the ritual words and begins the most solemn part of the meeting, in which the words our Lord said during the Last Supper are pronounced over the bread and wine.

From our perspective, what seems striking is the humiliation the poorest must have felt at this way of proceeding. In that context, however, not everyone would have seen it that way. It was not at all unusual in that society, at a dinner, for different qualities of food and drink to be served according to the different social status of the guests.[57] In such a stratified

---

[57] A letter of Pliny the Younger (61–112 CE), dated at the beginning of the second century, gives us a good idea of this. The author describes to

society as that, it could seem "normal" that those who belonged to the upper classes would have more and better food than the others, even in the context of a meal in common.[58]

Paul finds this unacceptable and uses harsh language to condemn this way of acting: "Whoever eats and drinks without discerning the body, eats and drinks a judgment against themselves" (1 Cor 11:29). It is clear that "discerning the body" does not refer to recognizing the bread and wine as the Body and Blood of Christ; what is at stake here is not transubstantiation or the real presence. The error of the Corinthians was not to understand the relationship between the bread and wine and the *ekklēsia* that incarnates the Body of Christ.

The wealthy Christians of Corinth, by clinging to the privileges that their status conferred on them, became incapable of seeing the new reality that the Risen Christ had inaugurated and of which the *ekklēsia* was the sign: a reconciled humanity in which the wounds caused by social and economic inequalities were beginning to be healed. Their humiliating behavior was more than discourtesy, because it made them "guilty with respect to the body and blood of the Lord" (1 Cor 11:27), which is like saying accomplices of "those who were responsible for the crucifixion, and not among those who by faith receive the fruit of it."[59]

Paul was realistic. He neither claimed to eliminate all at once the serious inequalities of Roman society, nor did he command the rich Christians of Corinth to renounce their possessions.

---

a friend a dinner at which he had just taken part as the guest of honor: "The host had prepared plentiful delicacies for himself and for a few others, and distasteful and meager things to eat for the others. He also distributed wine in small cups, distinguishing three types, not to allow people to choose, but so that there was no way to refuse: one for him and for me, a second for his less intimate friends (since he divides his friends into different classes), and a third for his and my freedmen." *Letters*, II, 6, 2.

[58] J. D. G. Dunn, *The Theology of Paul the Apostle*, 610.

[59] C. K. Barrett, *A Commentary on the First Epistle to the Corinthians*, London 1968, 273.

But he was intransigent in maintaining the vitality of a dynamism able to transform deeply the character of persons and of the community—the practice of sacramental sharing that ensured that relationships characteristic of the Kingdom would begin to take shape and become a reality.

We have here the only New Testament text that describes the Eucharist in detail, and it does so in order to condemn an abuse.[60] Paul does not criticize the lack of respect towards the sacramental species or the absence of decorum of the celebration; the fault of the Corinthians was rather to sabotage the social dynamics of transformation set in motion by the celebration of the Lord's Supper. The Christ who shared his table with sinners, who fed a crowd of hungry people on the hills of Galilee, who sent out his apostles before his Passion, leaving them his Body as a legacy, calls together those who meet around the bread and wine so that they may be a leaven of reconciliation in a fragmented world. Eating without discerning the Body means refusing to change the kind of human relationships that eminent people and the leaders of the nations have imposed with their power.

The task of Christian ethics is nothing other than to show how to keep on celebrating the Eucharist by other means. In other words, how can we live without interrupting that process of transformation that we begin to experience when we share the Lord's Table in community?[61]

---

[60] Richard Hays states with humor: "Strangely, we are indebted to the Corinthians for messing up their celebrations of the Lord's Supper. If they had not suffered divisions at the Lord's Table, Paul would never have written to correct them, and we would know nothing about his teaching concerning the tradition and practice of the Lord's Supper. (And some New Testament scholars would undoubtedly insist that the Eucharist was unknown in the Pauline churches, since he does not mention it elsewhere in his surviving letters!)." *First Corinthians*, Louisville 1997, 203.

[61] One of the books of Christian ethics published in recent years is an ecumenical project that presents Christian ethics as a commentary on the different moments of the Eucharistic celebration: S. Hauerwas – S. Wells (eds.), *The Blackwell Companion to Christian Ethics*, Malden 2011.

Love in the *Polis*

In agreement with Aristotle, the virtues are acquired when citizens responsible for the destiny of their *polis* try to give the best of themselves in a collaborative project of organizing their life together. One of the great ironies of the history of the West is that it was precisely one of Aristotle's pupils, Alexander the Great, who ended the self-government of the city-states that were, according to the great philosopher, the hallmark of a fully human life.

On the death of Alexander (323 BCE), the immense empire that he conquered was divided among his generals and a new Greek-speaking culture prevailed in the eastern Mediterranean world. This civilization—called "Hellenism" by historians—perpetuated and internationalized the language and many of the artistic, intellectual and scientific achievements of classical Greece, but it eliminated the sovereignty and the form of civic life of the city-states. As time passed, territorial entities of larger dimensions displaced the *polis* as seats of power.

At the time of Christ and the first Christians, the Roman Empire had become the master of all the Mediterranean coast-lands. Hellenistic culture, however, continued basically unchanged, because the new rulers of the world liked Greek culture, which in addition facilitated the flow of riches to Rome. In this cultural and political climate, the Aristotelian ideal of happiness shared with other citizen-friends who held in their hands the destiny of the *polis* was no longer viable or credible. The new philosophical schools that arose in that context adapted themselves to the new situation.

Stoicism, for example, was rooted in a deterministic vision of the universe. Everything obeys an unswerving reason; freedom is an illusion, because in reality nothing that happens can take place in any other way. The only happiness possible for human beings lies in making one's ego a fortress; the supreme virtue is *ataraxia*, not letting oneself be affected by anything.

Epicureanism, on the contrary, claimed that everything happens by chance. Reality is the result of atoms that assemble and disassemble randomly; no transcendent reason governs the way things occur. The only intelligent thing one can do in a world lacking in any design is to try and minimize suffering and maximize pleasure.

Cynicism, for its part, gambled on radicalism. With its provocative behavior, it challenged conventional values and denounced the absurdity of life in society.

In this cultural situation, in which the best thinkers advised people to leave the public realm and make happiness a private question, Christianity defended concern for the common good and its necessity. Its proposal was not to recover and promote it by means of a philosophical discourse, but through a community in which it became possible to experience the happiness of sharing the mission entrusted by a good God. Those who met weekly in small assemblies in the different cities of the Empire understood themselves as having a "citizenship in heaven" (*politeuma en ouranois*, Phil 3:20; cf. 1:27), cells of a political project that would be fully realized at the end of time, but whose form of life could already be tasted here on earth.

Christians did not enter politics in the sense that they had a plan to gain power, but their proposal was political in another sense: recuperating the social space as a place to grow as persons. Christians nourished the hope that it was possible to achieve happiness by sharing the project of building a universal brotherhood/sisterhood, a hope against all hope, because the Empire in which they lived was both powerful and hostile. They trusted in "the surpassing greatness of [God's] might on behalf of those who believe, in conformity with the working of his mighty power, which he put to work in Christ by raising him from the dead and seating him at his right hand in the heavens, far above every ruler and authority and power and dominion" (Eph 1:19-21).

Hospitality, works of mercy, the celebration of the Eucharist, and the other Christian practices realized in community were the means by which God was transforming both them and the world. The happiness to which they aspired was not material abundance or power, but becoming like Jesus, a man whose character could be described by the Beatitudes. They understood that their lives were part of a larger story: the story of salvation that, with infinite patience, God was working out in the world.

❖   ❖   ❖

The question of Christian ethics today is, in essence, the same as it was then: How can we Christians become what God wants us to be in his plan of salvation, realizing that this becoming is inseparable from the way we live our lives in concrete terms?

The question is the same, but not the answers, because the forms of life depend on the circumstances of each culture and each historical moment. Today as before we must take into account the church, a concrete community that has kept alive the project of Jesus across the centuries. It is clear that Christians are no longer a marginal group that survives clandestinely under the watchful eye of the Roman Empire. After the unexpected access to the circles of power that the Constantinian shift made possible, its history became complicated and ambiguous—like life itself. Today many people do not believe that Christians, divided as we are into many denominations and burdened with all sorts of scandals, can contribute anything to human progress. But those who believe in the first beatitude, "Happy the poor in spirit," hope that the Lord will make of our poor selves instruments of his plan for the world.

In our day, few people associate "love" and "politics." Even more, they imagine that the proper domain of love is the couple or the family, which in contemporary culture are seen as a refuge from life in heartless cities where the struggle of interests and sordid games predominate. The vocation of the church is precisely to break with this privatized outlook and to present itself as the social space that enables persons of different social, economic and cultural backgrounds to live as brothers and sisters. When the church is a sign of unity in pluralism, it becomes possible to learn in her to love those who are not like us and to educate ourselves in *philoxenia*, love of someone different.

Earlier we quoted two ethically luminous verses: "Abide in brotherly love (*philadelphia*); do not neglect hospitality (*philoxenia*)" (Heb 13:1-2). We believe that the greatest moral urgency for Christians today is to create spaces of community participation in which it is possible to exercise a fraternal sharing (*philadelphia*) open to welcoming those who are different (*philoxenia*). Perhaps in this way Christianity could go from being a "religion," in other words a system of norms and beliefs, to understanding itself as a network of friends involved in a common creation: God's project to reconcile with himself, with themselves and with one another all human beings.

If, even very precariously, Christians managed to bring to life these kinds of communities, we would situate ourselves in this space and in this time where the Spirit does not cease to illuminate new paths for humanity.

Epilogue

A thousand years ago, Anselm of Canterbury defined theology as *fides quaerens intellectum*, faith seeking understanding. Christian ethics is theology reflecting on the essentially practical character of this faith.[1]

In this sense, being a believer does not consist principally in accepting as true a certain number of propositions, but in responding with one's life to the God who revealed himself in Jesus Christ. Moral theology is at the service of this process in which convictions and conduct are interrelated.

By means of three categories—happiness, virtue and love—we have reflected on three of the basic affirmations of Christian life.

The first affirmation can be expressed in this way: *The revelation of the triune God places human life in the horizon of an intentionality*. Existence acquires meaning when we discover that it has a purpose, and this purpose lies in placing ourselves at the service of the Reign of God, that enters the world in Jesus and that the Spirit continues to bring about with our assistance. Happiness, for Christians, means taking part in this story (chapter 4).

The second affirmation is: *Happiness belongs to the realm of being*. As a result, being happy does not mean possessing

---

[1] According to Stanley Hauerwas, "Ethics is but a name for exposing the practical character of theological speech," *Hannah's Child: A Theologian's Memoir*, Grand Rapids 2010, 237.

wealth, enjoying pleasures or becoming famous; in other words it is not rooted in *having* an external good. Being happy is rather learning to *be* in a certain way. In this sense, the virtues describe the character traits of a happy person, which are synthesized in the Beatitudes (chapter 5). They are the list of virtues, the moral characteristics that Jesus himself proposed to his followers as a model of happiness.

The third and final is: *We undertake this journey towards virtue in community*. The loving project of Jesus has been embodied from the very beginning in a community of brothers and sisters. The friendship among those who share the Christian vocation (*philadelphia*) must always be open to the "other" (*philoxenia*). The project of universal brotherhood/sisterhood in God becomes real in the mutual love of a concrete community that is open to all through hospitality and service (chapter 6).

These three affirmations, which form the basis of the Christian moral grammar, exist in a reciprocal relationship. According to this outlook, it is meaningful to *be* in a certain way, since the project of Jesus requires a certain kind of person. Still more, we cultivate certain *virtues*, because the *goal* we are striving after has need of them.

At the same time, this *goal* is also contained seminally in the *virtues*, because the happiness to which we aspire is a form of being: the Kingdom is not a state of things but rather a state of persons and relationships. It comes into being when men and women change their form of being and begin to treat one another differently.

In addition, there is a reciprocal relationship between *purpose* and *community*, between happiness and love. The Christian community arises as a human response to the revelation of the triune God. The project of the Kingdom creates fellow travelers, but the end is already contained as a seed in the community that comes together to realize it. The church is a parable of the Kingdom on earth when the love among its members is sincere and widens to welcome those wounded by life.

And finally, *virtues* and *community* exist in a mutual relationship. We cannot acquire the form of being characterized by the virtues without a community in which we learn poverty of spirit, non-violence, mercy, purity of heart, etc. We receive the spirit of the Beatitudes through the church, but the church is sustained in its turn by this form of being, because without persons transformed by the Spirit, all that remains of it is its institutional shell. When the virtues are lacking, we end up turning to rules that exclude in order to maintain the illusion of a "Christian identity."

The purpose of this book has been simply to sketch out a *Moral Grammar of the New Testament*. I hope that I have helped the reader to understand how these three "grammatical rules" serve as the basis for a language adapted to express the Gospel. Without these three pillars—purpose, transformation of being and community—the Christian "language" becomes unintelligible. But by putting together the three, we can express today as well the hope of the Kingdom in a multitude of forms.

It goes without saying that what has been attempted here is only an *Introduction* to Christian ethics. We have remained at the threshold of the tasks that constitute the content of moral theology: the difficult discernments that the concrete realization of Christian practices requires in our day.

Alasdair MacIntyre reminds us that a practice is a complex form of human activity in which the models of excellence towards which we aspire change in every epoch.[2] Christian practices are not an exception: they are rooted in Tradition, but precisely because this Tradition is living, they aspire to take shape in a new way in every historical epoch. In this sense, Christian ethics is called to be the "department of research, development and innovation" of a community that knows that the project of Jesus must confront new challenges in every generation. How can we practice hospitality today in a global-

[2] A. C. MacIntyre, *After Virtue: A Study in Moral Theory*, Notre Dame IN, 2007, 187.

ized world with massive movements of population? How can
we work for peace on a planet threatened by the disharmony
of climate change? How can the church be a "field hospital"
for those who are suffering from broken relationships and
abandonment?[3] These and so many other questions do not
require a code of rules, but above all the hope that creative
proposals rooted in the living Tradition can bring.[4]

Since the Second Vatican Council, moral theology has
emerged as a new discipline, leaving behind the casuistic
model in which it had been pigeonholed. This change, however, does not exempt it from dealing with urgent questions
situated in social and cultural contexts that are becoming more
and more complex. For example, under what conditions
should we suspend intensive treatment of a premature infant
if we want to honor this being as a member of our human
family? Can a Christian charitable association accept donations
from a bank that is responsible for evictions, when that money
will go to alleviate the effects of those evictions? How can we
welcome a person married in the church who is awakening
for the first time to a personal relationship with Christ just as
he begins to become aware of his homosexual orientation? And
so on. The extraordinary sensitivity for nuances that moral
theology has developed across the centuries is shown to be a
treasure whose contribution we cannot do without today.

Joseph Ratzinger wrote: "This process [of moral discern-
ment] cannot be carried out in every detail by an isolated Magisterium, with oracular infallibility. The life and suffering of
Christians who profess their faith in the midst of their times

---

[3] The expression "field hospital" was used by Pope Francis to refer to
the church. *La Civiltà Cattolica*, September 2013, https://www.thepope
speaks.com/the-church-as-field-hospital/.

[4] Yves Congar spoke of the criterion of "faithfulness to the future" for
every creative proposal that is offered in the church, always in harmony
with the authentic tradition. Cf. Brother Emile of Taizé, *Faithful to the
Future: Listening to Yves Congar*, London 2013.

have just as important a part to play as the thinking and questioning of the learned, which would have a very hollow ring without the backing of Christian existence, which learns to discern spirits in the travail of everyday life."[5]

The church is a diverse community of men and women, and all of them are necessary to realize the discernments indispensable to go forward with the project of the Kingdom. Moral theology has to be a service meant especially for those communities and persons who are reflecting on ways of contributing to the new thing that the Spirit is attempting to awaken in the difficult conditions of a culture in crisis. In this sense, its first task consists in listening, in a special way, to those involved in the stresses and strains of daily life.

Jesus said, "Not everyone who says to me 'Lord, Lord' will enter the Kingdom of heaven, but the one who does the will of my Father in heaven" (Matt 7:21). In the last section of the Sermon on the Mount, Christ insists in different ways that his words have to be brought to life (Matt 7:13-29). When he says farewell to his followers at the end of this same gospel, he says, "Go, then, and make disciples of all nations, baptizing them in the Name of the Father and the Son and the Holy Spirit, teaching them to put into practice all I have commanded you" (Matt 28:19-20). We have tried to situate Christian ethics in the context of this mission.

---

[5] J. Ratzinger, "Magisterium of the Church, Faith, Morality," in C. E. Curran – R. A. McCormick (eds.), *Readings in Moral Theology. No. 2: The Distinctiveness of Christian Ethics*, New York 1980, 186.

Annotated Bibliography

Aristotle, *The Nichomachean Ethics,* **Oxford 2009.**
The oldest ethical treatise of the Western tradition is also a permanent reference for all who wish to think about moral behavior in our culture. Speaking of ethics without being acquainted with it is like speaking of Spanish literature without having read *Don Quixote.*

Alasdair C. MacIntyre, *After Virtue: A Study in Moral Theory,* **Notre Dame IN 2007 (third edition).**
This book of MacIntyre's (1929–) is probably the main cause of the "return to Aristotle" that has taken place in philosophy and theology over the past three decades. His profound critique of the philosophies that are the basis of modernity leads him to emphasize the necessity for ethics to speak of ends and not just means. Even if one does not agree with his most radical conclusions, reading him is a constant provocation to rethink the ideas that lie at the root of contemporary culture.

Amartya Sen, *On Ethics and Economics,* **Oxford/New York 1987.**
Nobel Prize winner for Economics in 1998 for his contributions to the study of famines, human welfare and the factors underlying poverty, Sen (1933–) introduced the category of "human capability" as a corrective to a vision of development based solely on the maximization of utility. In this book he attempts to reconcile his vision of ethics—with Aristotelian overtones—and the science of economics.

Bernhard Häring, *Free and Faithful in Christ: Moral Theology for Clergy and Laity,* **3 vols., New York 1979.**
Häring (1912–1998) is probably the theologian who did the most for the renewal of Catholic moral theology before, during and after the

Second Vatican Council. This three-volume work is his great post-conciliar book (before the council he wrote his other masterpiece, *The Law of Christ*). Chapter 2 of the first volume (pp. 28–58) offers a panorama of the history of Catholic moral reflection from the church fathers until the twentieth century.

Herbert Vorgrimler (dir.), *Commentary on the Documents of Vatican II*, 5 vols., New York-London 1969.

Joseph Ratzinger, Alois Grillmeier and Béda Rigaux wrote a commentary on the constitution *Dei Verbum* (vol. II, pp. 497–583 in the German original and vol. III, pp. 155–272 in the English translation). Their reflections help us to understand the faith of the Catholic Church and placed the Bible once again at the center of its life. Particularly brilliant are the pages written by a then-young German theologian, Joseph Ratzinger (1927–).

Roger Schutz – Max Thurian, *Revelation, a Protestant View: The Dogmatic Constitution on Divine Revelation, a Commentary*, Westminster MD 1968.

Brother Roger (1915–2005), founder of the ecumenical Community of Taizé, and one of his brothers, Max (1921–1996), were present at the Second Vatican Council as observers. This commentary on the constitution *Dei Verbum* from a Protestant viewpoint is a little jewel—today almost forgotten—of ecumenical sensitivity. The English version has a prologue by Henri de Lubac.

Pontifical Biblical Commission, *The Bible and Morality: Biblical Roots of Christian Conduct*, Vatican City 2008, http://www.vatican.va/roman_curia/congregations/cfaith/pcb _documents/rc_con_cfaith_doc_20080511_bibbia-e-morale _en.html.

The Pontifical Bible Commission worked for six years (2002–2008) to prepare this document, which expresses the position of this commission of the Congregation for the Doctrine of the Faith on the relationship between the Bible and morality. The first part speaks of Christian behavior as a response to the gift of God; the second proposes criteria of moral discernment that can be found in the Bible.

Charles E. Curran – Richard A. McCormick (eds.), *Readings in Moral Theology. No. 2: The Distinctiveness of Christian Ethics,* **New York 1980.**
The last great "clash of schools" in moral theology took place in the 1970s between the "Autonomy School" and the "Ethics of Faith" (*Glaubensethik*). Both groups argued passionately about the specificity of Christian ethics. This volume contains articles from the most important authors on both sides of the debate.

Dietrich Bonhoeffer, *Ethics,* **New York 1995.**
A posthumous work of the great theologian of resistance against Nazism. Bonhoeffer (1906–1945) was working on this book when he was arrested and, after several months in prison, executed. In this work he tried to respond to what he believed was the most urgent challenge that Christian thought had to confront: articulating a theological ethics that could help the church to be a prophetic sign for the world.

Stanley Hauerwas, *The Peaceable Kingdom: A Primer in Christian Ethics,* **Notre Dame 1983.**
Hauerwas (1940–), called "America's best theologian" by Time Magazine, continues Bonhoeffer's idea of proposing a *theological ethics* that can help the church to be a prophetic presence in a world that, although no longer subject to Nazi terror, suffers from fragmentation and violence in old and new ways. The work of Hauerwas is vast; this is a good place to begin.

Stanley Hauerwas – Samuel Wells (eds.), *The Blackwell Companion to Christian Ethics,* **Malden 2011.**
Theologians of different confessions, many of them disciples and friends of Hauerwas, present Christian life in this book as a continuation of the Eucharist by other means. Each part of the liturgical celebration is commented on in a chapter that reflects on its ethical implications, which go from the morality of the family to ecology.

John H. Yoder, *Body Politics: Five Practices of the Christian Community before the Watching World,* **Harrisonburg 2001.**
Mennonite communities try to live the commandments of Jesus in the Sermon on the Mount in a radical fashion, especially those regarding

the refusal of violence. Yoder (1927–1997) is the theologian who put on the map at the end of the twentieth century the theology of this church community, often persecuted in the course of history by Christians of other confessions. This small book studies how five practices that are described in the New Testament can be lived out today—the power of binding and loosing, the Lord's Supper, baptism, charisms and prophecy.

Julie Hanlon Rubio, *Family Ethics: Practices for Christians*, Washington DC 2010.

The use of the category "practice" to articulate moral theology is very promising. This American Catholic theologian, married and with three children, is a professor at St. Louis University. In this book she explains family ethics, not through norms or principles, but following five practices—sexual faithfulness, eating together, tithing, volunteering, and prayer.

Rudolf Schnackenburg, *The Moral Teaching of the New Testament*, New York 1964.

Schnackenburg (1914–2002), considered the most important German Catholic exegete of the twentieth century, is the author of this fundamental book for the study of New Testament ethics. Based on a historical reconstruction of the context of Jesus and the biblical authors, he studies in the New Testament the basic characteristics of its moral teaching. The treatment of some key themes, such as Jesus's commandment to love or the concept of conscience in Paul, are outstanding.

Wayne A. Meeks, *The Moral World of the First Christians*, Philadelphia 1986.

Professor at Yale University, Wayne Meeks (1932–), attempts in this book to undertake an "ethnography" of early Christianity. He studies the New Testament and other ancient texts as if he were an anthropologist, to discover in them the practices that form the ecosystem of Christian life in the first two centuries. This description leads him to formulate a moral grammar of Christian practices that shows how each of them contributes to articulating a coherent language. One conclusion of this study is that to practice morality and to live as a community are part of one and the same dialectic process.

Richard B. Hays, *The Moral Vision of the New Testament: Community, Cross, New Creation; A Contemporary Introduction to New Testament Ethics,* **San Francisco 1996.**

This American Methodist exegete, a professor at Duke University, does not restrict himself to describing the moral behavior of the first Christians, but attempts to present the relevance of the New Testament for contemporary moral questions. After a long hermeneutical excursus starting from the bible texts, he reflects on five contemporary moral questions—violence to defend justice, divorce and remarriage, homosexuality, anti-Semitism, and abortion. Even when one does not agree with all his conclusions, the hermeneutical process he employs must be taken into account.

Daniel J. Harrington – James F. Keenan, *Jesus and Virtue Ethics: Building Bridges between New Testament Studies and Moral Theology,* **Lanham 2002.**

Two American Jesuit theologians, one of them a bible scholar—Harrington—and the other a moral theologian—Keenan—are the authors of this book that does what its title claims: building a bridge between the New Testament and moral theology, by means of a study of the life and teaching of Jesus through the lens of virtue-ethics.

N. T. Wright, *Virtue Reborn,* **London 2010. (American edition:** *After You Believe: Why Christian Character Matters,* **New York 2012.)**

An Anglican bishop and theologian, Tom Wright (1948–) is one of the most erudite living Christian exegetes and one with the most to say. His immense work is based on a careful historical study of the New Testament that, despite his attention to detail, never loses sight of the larger questions. In this book, written for the general reader, the author uses virtue-ethics to describe the Christian life reflected in the New Testament.

Ulrich Luz, *Matthew 1–7: A Commentary (revised),* **Minneapolis 2007.**

In my opinion, this is the best commentary on Matthew's gospel available in any language. Not only does it analyze the meaning of the passages in their original historical context, but it presents how the gospel passages have been interpreted throughout the following centuries until today. A very important reference for studying the Sermon on the Mount in detail.

John de Taizé, *Friends in Christ: Paths to a New Understanding of Church*, Maryknoll 2012.

Following Brother Roger of Taizé, who stated that "Christ did not come to earth to start a new religion, but to offer to every human being a communion in God," Brother John proposes an understanding of the church as a "multitude of friends" engaged in Jesus's proposal to create a universal family. A book born of the experience of welcoming the tens of thousands of young people who flock to the hill of Taizé each year.

Horst Balz – Gerhard Schneider (eds.), *Exegetical Dictionary of the New Testament*, 3 vols., Grand Rapids 1990.

The most useful biblical dictionary available. If someone wants to know in depth the meaning of a Greek term used in the New Testament, this is the place to go.